Table of Contents

Introduction

Thank you for purchasing this study guide for the Certification Foundation and CIPP/US examinations administered by the International Association of Privacy Professionals ("IAPP"). By purchasing this guide, you have taken the first step to passing the exams and becoming a certified privacy professional!

Before you begin working your way through this guide, you should be aware of how it is organized. This guide is divided into two parts: the first covering the Certification Foundation exam and the second covering the CIPP/US exam. Each part begins with a condensed text that discusses core privacy principles, which is then followed by an extensive set of sample questions with detailed answers. Although working through sample questions is the best way to study for the exams, you will also need a thorough understanding of core privacy principles. This guide provides you with both. The condensed text provides you with the fundamentals of privacy law, while the sample questions reinforce and supplement your knowledge.

Each chapter of this guide also begins with a list of important terms relevant to the subject matter discussed in that chapter. Definitions of these terms can be found in the IAPP's glossary located at:

http://www.cippexam.com/glossary

You should read the definition provided for each term several times. Many questions on the exam come directly from the glossary, and therefore it is important that you thoroughly understand the meaning of these important terms.

Finally, please remember to carefully read the sample questions and answers provided at the end of each part of this guide. In some cases, the questions test subject matter not fully disclosed in the condensed text portions of this guide. The sample questions are designed to supplement the material contained in the text. It is therefore important that you read the questions and answers several times so that you completely understand the concepts being tested.

By systematically working your way through this guide, you will have all the information necessary to pass both the Certification Foundation and CIPP/US exams on your very first try.

Good Luck!

About the Certification Foundation Examination

The Certification Foundation examination is the gateway to all of IAPP's certifications. The exam covers the fundamental principles of information privacy and protection from a global perspective.

To receive a certification from the IAPP, a candidate must successfully pass the Certification Foundation exam and one other specialty exam, including CIPP/US, CIPP/C, CIPP/E, CIPP/G, CIPP/IT, CIPM, and CIPT.

The Certification Foundation exam is a 100 minute, 105 item, objective (that is, multiple-choice) test. There are no essay questions, and each correct answer is worth one point. The exam includes 90 scored items and 15 non-scored, trial items. You will not know which questions are scored when taking the exam, and therefore you should treat all questions as if they are scored.

Also, you are not penalized for incorrect answers. Therefore, a general exam taking strategy is to answer every question on the exam, even those you are unsure of. Eliminate obviously incorrect answers and then choose the best answer remaining. Do not leave any questions unanswered.

Lastly, on a more personal note, be sure to give yourself adequate time to prepare for the examination. This guide is quite lengthy, and you will need several weeks (at a minimum) to work through all of the material. Take your time and absorb the material. You will not obtain a firm grasp of the information contained in this guide by simply skimming it. Carefully read the sample questions as well as the detailed answers. You will likely see dozens of questions on your exam that test the same subject matter as our sample questions. If you answer these questions correctly, you are well on your way to becoming a certified privacy professional!

Chapter 1: Fundamental Privacy Principles

This chapter addresses common themes and principles to information privacy in the United States and overseas. You should expect anywhere from 31 to 35 questions on your examination testing subject matter covered in this chapter.

A. Glossary Terms

It is important that you thoroughly understand fundamental privacy principles before taking the exam because of the relatively high number of questions testing the fundamentals. Therefore, you should carefully read the definitions provided in the glossary for the important terms listed below. The glossary is located at:

http://www.cippexam.com/glossary

Glossary Terms: Accountability, APEC Privacy Principles, Bodily Privacy, Choice, Closed Circuit Television, Collection Limitation, Communications Privacy, Consent, Customer Information, Data Controller, Data Elements, Data Processor, Data Protection Directive, Data Quality, Data Subject, De-identification, European Convention for the Protection of Human Rights and Fundamental Freedoms, Fair Credit Reporting Act, Fair Information Practices, Four Classes of Privacy, Individual Participation, Information Lifecycle, Information Privacy, International Data Transfers, Internet Protocol Address, Internet Service Provider, Jurisdiction, Madrid Resolution, Minimum Necessary Requirement, Negligence, OECD Guidelines, Openness, Opt-in, Opt-out, Organization for Economic Cooperation and

Development, Personal Data, Personal Information, Privacy Assessment, Privacy by Design, Privacy Impact Assessment, Privacy Notice, Privacy Policy, Public Records, Publicly Available Information, Purpose Specification, Retention, Right to Privacy, Security Safeguards, Special Categories of Data, Territorial Privacy, Universal Declaration of Human Rights, Use Limitation.

B. Definition of Privacy

Privacy has been defined in many ways. For example, some view privacy as the fundamental right to be left alone. Others define privacy as the right of an individual to be protected against intrusion into his personal life or affairs by direct physical means or by publication of information.

In general, all definitions of privacy revolve around the notion that society should respect an individual's autonomy, and an individual should be free from unreasonable intrusion on that autonomy from both the government and private parties. No matter how one defines privacy, there remains a universal and almost innate understanding of the importance of privacy and privacy protection. Accordingly, many diverse regions and cultures today recognize privacy rights.

C. Types of Privacy

Privacy can be divided into four main types or areas. Each type is related, but a separate and distinct framework has developed for analyzing each area.

The four types of privacy are:

1. Information privacy: concerned with the collection and handling of personal data, such as credit information and medical records. The focus of the Certification Foundation exam is on principles associated with information privacy.

2. Bodily privacy: involves protection of an individual's physical being and includes issues such as genetic testing and drug testing.

3. Communication privacy: encompasses the security and confidentiality of all types of correspondence, including email, postal mail, telephone and fax communications, as well as ordinary verbal communications.

4. Territorial privacy: concerned with intrusion into an individual's environment (for example, an individual's home or workplace) and addresses issues such as video surveillance and identification checks.

Figure 1 on the following page depicts the four main types of privacy. You will likely see several questions on your exam testing whether you know the four types of privacy and the basic characteristics of each type.

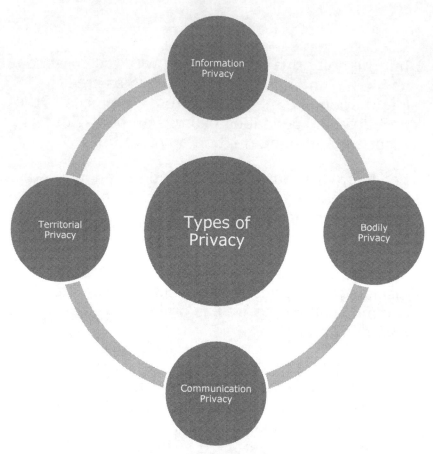

Figure 1: Types of Privacy

D. Types of Information

For privacy purposes, all information can be classified as either (1) personal information or (2) non-personal information. Personal information has been given different labels across the globe. For example, countries in the European Union ("EU") generally use the term "personal data" to describe personal information. In the United States, the term "personally identifiable information" (or "PII") is typically used. Canada simply uses "personal information" in its core privacy law, which is titled the Personal Information Protection and Electronic Documents Act ("PIPEDA"). This guide uses the terms "personal information" and "personal data" interchangeably.

The meaning of personal information, regardless of which label is used, is the same. Personal information is any information (including both paper and electronic records) that relates to or describes an <u>identified or identifiable individual</u>. Consequently, information about a corporation is not personal information because it does not relate to an individual.

The dividing line between personal and non-personal information is sometimes not clear. For example, a specific job title may uniquely identify a person (for example, chief executive officer). However, some titles are not very specific (for example, associate) and may apply to hundreds, if not thousands, of people at an organization.

When determining whether information is personal information, a good rule of thumb is to examine how uniquely the information describes a person. Information that is unique to a specific person or small group of persons is more likely to constitute personal information. Applying this principle, the human resources data elements "department" and "title" are typically not considered personal information because they relate to a potentially large group of people. In contrast, "salary" and other more uniquely identifying data, such as performance evaluations, are generally classified as personal information.

Certain types of important personal information may be further classified as "sensitive" personal information. What constitutes sensitive personal information differs from one jurisdiction to another. For example, Article 8 of the EU Data Protection Directive defines sensitive data, which is called "special categories of data," as information that reveals racial origin, political opinions, religious or philosophical beliefs, trade-union membership, or data concerning health or sex life. In the United States, Social Security numbers are generally considered sensitive personal data. In virtually all jurisdictions, health-related data, such as prescribed medications and medical diagnoses, constitutes sensitive personal information because they relate to the inner workings of one's body and mind, which is inherently private and sensitive.

Non-personal information is all data that does not relate to an identified or identifiable individual. For example, data that has been "anonymized," "de-identified" or "aggregated" for research or statistical purposes is non-personal information. As previously discussed, data concerning an organization is also not personal information unless the data can be clearly linked to an individual (for example, when the company is a sole proprietorship).

You will likely see several questions on the Certification Foundation exam testing the distinction between personal and non-personal information. Therefore, it is important that you readily understand the difference. Again, personal information is all information that relates to or describes an identified or identifiable individual. Information relating to a company, such as a corporate financial report, is non-personal information. Similarly, data that is no longer reasonably linked to an identifiable person, such as anonymized or de-identified research data, is also non-personal information.

Privacy laws typically only regulate the processing of personal information. Non-personal data may be processed without restriction. Therefore, it is important to initially determine whether personal information is being processed when analyzing a fact pattern appearing on the Certification Foundation exam. Correctly classifying the data as either personal or non-personal information is an important first step in all privacy-related problems.

E. Sources of Information

There are three main sources of information. They include:

1. Public records: information collected and maintained by the government and available to the public. Examples of public records include real estate deeds, birth and marriage certificates, tax liens, and other data recorded by the government and made available for public inspection.

2. Publicly available information: data, in any form, that is generally accessible to the interested public. Examples of publicly available information include information contained in newspapers, research articles, books and other publications, as well as information obtained through Internet searches.

3. Non-public information: data that has not been made available to the public. Examples of non-public information include a company's trade

secrets, as well as business plans and strategy related documents of an organization.

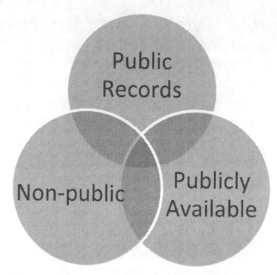

Figure 2: Sources of Information

As shown in Figure 2, information may be derived from more than one source. For example, a public company's financial data is generally non-public information before an earnings call, publicly available information after an earnings call or press release containing the information, and a public record once it is formally included as part of a Securities and Exchange Commission ("SEC") report.

It is important to consider the source of personal information because the source will dictate how the information may be used. For example, personal data obtained from public records can generally be used without restriction, whereas personal data obtained from non-public sources typically cannot be used unless permission is first obtained.

For the most part, privacy laws only protect personal information obtained from non-public sources. In other words, privacy laws typically do not protect non-personal information or even personal information obtained from public sources. If personal information from a non-public source is involved, then various legal, regulatory, and contractual provisions may govern the use of that information. Accordingly, two threshold questions are very important when analyzing a privacy-related problem: (1) does the data constitute personal information and (2) from what source was the data obtained. A plethora of legal rights and obligations will attach to activities involving personal information from non-public sources, as explained later in this guide.

F. Entities that Process Personal Information

Most privacy laws regulate the "processing" of personal information. Virtually any activity performed on or with personal information is considered processing. Examples of processing include collection, recording, organization, storage, alteration, retrieval, consultation, use, disclosure, dissemination, blocking, erasure, and destruction. Processing also encompasses both manual and automated or computerized means of performing these activities.

Three main parties are typically involved in the processing of personal information. They include:

1. Data controller: the person or entity that determines, alone or jointly with others, the purposes and the means of the processing of personal data;

2. Data processor: the person or entity that processes personal data on behalf of the controller; and

3. <u>Data subject</u>: the person about whom the personal data relates or describes.

For example, if a hospital collects personal information about its patients and transfers the personal information to a third party responsibly for billing the patients, the hospital is the data controller, the biller is the data processor, and the patients are the data subjects.

A fourth party may also sometimes be involved in the processing of personal information. For example, personal data may be imported to or exported from a particular country. In that case, the data importer or exporter may have certain rights and obligations under the applicable laws of the importing or exporting country. Therefore, the data importer or exporter may be a fourth party involved in the processing of personal information.

When analyzing fact patterns on the Certification Foundation exam, it is useful to identify each of these parties and determine what rights and responsibilities each party has under the applicable privacy rule, regulation, or law.

G. Privacy Policies and Notices

Although many people use the terms "privacy policy" and "privacy notice" interchangeably, these two terms actually represent two distinct statements.

A <u>privacy policy</u> is an internal statement that describes an organization's information handling practices and procedures. It is directed to the employees and agents of the organization.

A privacy notice, on the other hand, is an external statement that is directed to an organization's potential and actual customers or users. It describes how the organization will process personal information. The privacy notice also typically describes the options a data subject has with respect to the organization's processing of his personal information (e.g., the opportunity to "opt out"). It is common for an organization to use its privacy policy as a privacy notice. For example, an organization may publish its privacy notice on its website and rebrand the notice as a privacy policy.

The distinction between a privacy policy and a private notice is often tested on the Certification Foundation exam. In addition, many incorrect answers on the exam will use these terms incorrectly. For example, if an answer choice implies that a privacy policy is used as an external statement to inform customers about an organization's privacy practices, it is not likely the correct answer. On the exam, "privacy policy" and "privacy notice" represent two distinct statements. Again, a privacy policy is an internal statement, while a privacy notice is an external statement. This makes intuitive sense because policies are generally internal operating documents, while notices are typically external announcements. You should remember this important distinction between the two statements.

H. Data Controls and Risk Assessment

Generally, there are three types of controls or safeguards that an organization may use to manage and protect personal information.

They include:

1. Administrative safeguards: management related policies or procedures for protecting personal information. An incident management plan and a privacy policy are two examples of administrative safeguards.

2. Physical safeguards: mechanisms that physically protect or prevent access to a resource. Examples of physical safeguards include cable locks for laptops and security guards for preventing unauthorized access to a building.

3. Technical safeguards: information technology measures that protect personal information. Examples of technical safeguards include password authentication schemes, encryption, and smart cards.

Companies should utilize all three types of safeguards (that is, administrative, physical, and technical) to protect sensitive personal information. Non-sensitive personal information should be protected by a combination of these three safeguards. Which specific safeguards or controls to use should depend on the importance of the information and the degree of risk associated with processing the information.

Managing risk associated with the processing of personal information is an important responsibility of an organization. Several tools exist to help an organization manage its data processing risk.

First, a privacy impact assessment ("PIA") is a systematic process for identifying the potential privacy related risks of a proposed system. When conducting a PIA, an organization analyzes how information is collected, stored, protected, shared, and managed to ensure that an organization has consciously incorporated privacy protection measures throughout the entire lifecycle of the data. A PIA should be carried out whenever a new data processing system or project is proposed, or when revisions to existing data practices are planned.

Second, a privacy audit or assessment is a systematic examination of an organization's compliance with its privacy policy and procedures, applicable laws and regulations, and other agreements and contracts concerning personal information. Audits should be conducted on a regular basis or at the request of a regulatory authority. Typically, privacy audits are performed by an internal taskforce of employees. However, when internal auditors are responsible for developing and implementing a privacy program, their independence may be impaired. For this reason, and due to the need for technical and legal expertise, third-party auditors may also be used.

Both privacy impact assessments and privacy audits are important tools that organizations should periodically use to manage their privacy-related risk.

I. The Information Lifecycle

All information, including personal information, undergoes a lifecycle at an organization. It is important to understand this lifecycle when developing a privacy policy that protects personal data throughout the various stages of its existence at an organization. As shown in Figure 3, the data lifecycle consists of (1) collection, (2) use, (3) disclosure, and (4) retention or destruction.

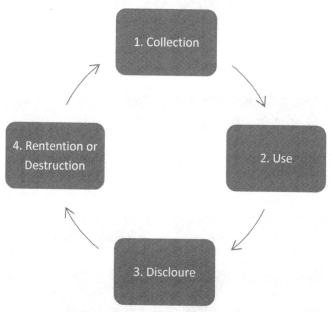

Figure 3: Information Lifecycle

A privacy policy should address an organization's information handling practices and procedures throughout the entire lifecycle from collection to retention or destruction of the information.

J. Fair Information Principles

The Fair Information Principles ("FIPs") are guidelines that represent widely-accepted doctrines concerning the fair processing of information. The FIPs serve as the building block of many international privacy initiatives, most notably the Guidelines on the Protection of Privacy and Transborder Flows of Personal Data adopted by the Organization for Economic Cooperation and Development in 1980 ("OECD Guidelines").

The core principles of privacy addressed by the FIPs are:

1. Notice and awareness: Consumers should be given notice of an organization's information practices before any personal information is collected from them;

2. Choice and consent: Consumers should have options to control how their data is used;

3. Access and participation: Consumers should have the ability to view, verify, and contest the accuracy of data collected about them;

4. Integrity and security: Organizations that collect data should ensure that the collected data is accurate and secure; and

5. Enforcement and redress: Enforcement measures, such as regulatory oversight with civil and/or criminal penalties for noncompliance, should be implemented to ensure that organizations follow the FIPs.

K. Types of Choice and Consent

There are two fundamental types of choice and consent that an organization may provide to a data subject. The first is called "opt-in" consent and the second is called "opt-out" consent.

Opt-in consent occurs when a data subject affirmatively and explicitly indicates his desire to have his data processed by an organization. For example, when data subjects expressly tells a data processor that certain specified types of processing are allowed on their data, they are opting in to the specified processing. Opt-in consent is sometimes referred to as affirmative consent.

Opt-out consent, on the other hand, occurs when data subjects implicitly consent by not indicating their disapproval of the requested processing. For example, if a data processor tells a data subject that his data will be processed in a particular way unless he notifies the processor within ten days, the processor is providing the data subject with the opportunity to opt out.

A good way to remember the difference between opt-in and opt-out consent is to consider what happens to a data subject's information if no action is taken. With opt-in consent, information is excluded from processing if the data subject does not act. With opt-out consent, information is included in processing if the data subject does not act.

In connection with online data processing, opt-in and opt-out consent can be illustrated with the web form on the following page.

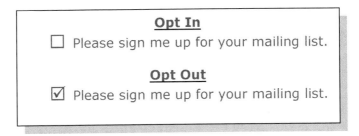

Figure 4: Opt In and Opt Out Illustration

With opt-in consent, the data subject must affirmatively check the box in order to join the organization's mailing list. The default action is that the data subject will not be added to the organization's mailing list. With opt-out consent, the box is pre-checked, and the data subject will join the mailing list unless he unselects the box. Thus, the default action is inclusion on the mailing list.

As will be described later in this guide, some types of processing will require a data subject to affirmatively opt in, while other types of processing require only opt-out consent. Opt-in consent is generally reserved for more intrusive processing, such as the transfer of sensitive personal information to third-parties, while opt-out consent is appropriate for less intrusive forms of processing, such as the sending of commercial emails to a recipient with an existing business relationship with the sender of the commercial emails.

Chapter 2: World Models of Data Protection and Industry Specific Privacy Laws

This chapter addresses the major privacy regimes throughout the world as well as privacy issues related to specific industries, such as the financial and healthcare industries. You should expect anywhere from 20 to 23 questions on your examination directed to subject matter from this chapter.

A. Glossary Terms

Your exam will contain a relatively high number of questions testing material from this chapter. Therefore, it is important that you read the definitions provided in the glossary for the important terms listed below. The glossary is located at:

http://www.cippexam.com/glossary

Glossary Terms: Act Respecting the Protection of Personal Information in the Private Sector, Adequate Level of Protection, Article 29 Working Party, Background Screening / Checks, Binding Corporate Rules, Canadian Standards Association, Children's Online Privacy Protection Act of 2000, Commercial Activity, Comprehensive Laws, Cookie, Cookie Directive, Co-regulatory Model, Data Processing, Data Protection Authority, Data Protection Commissioner, Data Protection Directive, Direct Marketing, Do Not Track, Employee Information, Encryption, European Economic Area, EU-U.S. Safe Harbor Agreement, European Commission, European Union, Fair Credit Reporting Act, Federal Trade Commission, Freedom of Information Act, Gramm-Leach-Bliley Act, Health Information Technology for Economic and Clinical

Heath Act, Health Insurance Portability and Accountability Act, Information Privacy, International Data Transfers, Medical Information, Non-public Personal information, PCI Data Security Standard, Personal Data, Personal Information, Personal Information Protection and Electronic Documents Act, Privacy Act of 1974, Public Records, Seal Programs, Sectoral Law / Model, Self-regulation Model, Smart Grid, Standard Model Clauses, Technology-based Model, WebTrust.

B. World Models of Privacy Protection

There are four major models of privacy protection used throughout the world. In most countries, several complementary models are employed simultaneously to effectively protect the privacy rights of individuals.

The four models are:

1. Comprehensive Model: In many countries, including those in the European Union ("EU"), there is a comprehensive or general law that governs the collection, use, and dissemination of personal information in both the private and public sectors. In countries employing a comprehensive model of privacy protection, an oversight body ensures compliance with the general privacy law. For example, each country in the EU has a national data protection authority responsible for ensuring compliance with the country's general privacy law, which is modeled after the EU Data Protection Directive.

2. Co-regulatory Model: A variant of the comprehensive model in which specific industries

develop rules for the protection of privacy within that industry that are enforced by the industry and overseen by a privacy agency. Canada, Australia, and New Zealand are three countries employing a co-regulatory model of privacy protection.

3. Sectoral Model: Some countries, including the United States and Japan, enact sector specific laws instead of a general data protection law. In these countries, enforcement is achieved through various mechanisms, including regulatory bodies, such as the Federal Trade Commission ("FTC") in the United States.

4. Self-regulatory Model: Industry associations establish rules or regulations that are adhered to by industry participants. Examples include the Payment Card Industry Data Security Standard ("PCI DSS") and the privacy seal programs administered by the Online Privacy Alliance. An organization's privacy policy is also a form of self-regulation.

In addition to the four major models discussed above, technology plays an important role in privacy protection. For example, Internet users may employ a wide range of technologic measures, such as software programs and hardware systems, to protect their privacy. These include encryption, digital signatures, anonymous remailers, firewalls, and proxy servers. Chapter 3 of this guide more fully addresses Internet privacy principles.

C. Overview of Major Privacy Initiatives

As previously discussed, the OECD Guidelines were adopted in 1980. The OECD Guidelines set forth eight privacy principles derived partly from the fair information principles ("FIPs"). These eight principles are:

1. Collection Limitation Principle: There should be limits to the collection of personal data and any collected data should be obtained by lawful and fair means and, where appropriate, with the knowledge or consent of the data subject;

2. Data Quality Principle: Personal data should be relevant to the purpose for which it is to be used, and it should be accurate, complete and kept up-to-date;

3. Purpose Specification Principle: The purpose for which personal data is collected should be specified at or before the time of data collection, and subsequent use should be limited to the fulfillment of that purpose or compatible purposes;

4. Use Limitation Principle: Personal data should not be disclosed or used for purposes other than those specified, except with the consent of the data subject or by the authority of law;

5. Security Safeguards Principle: Personal data should be protected by reasonable security safeguards against risk of loss or unauthorized access, destruction, use, modification, or disclosure;

6. Openness Principle: There should be a general policy of candor about developments, practices, and policies with respect to personal data.

Specifically, a data controller should be open and honest about the existence and nature of collected personal data, as well as the identity and residence of the data controller;

7. Individual Participation Principle: An individual should have the right to (a) obtain from a data controller confirmation of whether or not the data controller has data relating to him; (b) have communicated to him data relating to him within a reasonable time; at a charge, if any, that is not excessive; in a reasonable manner; and in a form that is readily intelligible to him; (c) be given reasons if a request is denied, and to be able to challenge such denial; and (d) challenge the accuracy of data relating to him and, if the challenge is successful, to have the data erased, rectified, completed, or amended; and

8. Accountability Principle: A data controller should be accountable for complying with measures that effectuate the principles stated above.

In 1995, the EU adopted Directive 95/46/EC ("EU Data Protection Directive"), which addressed the protection of individuals with regard to the processing of their personal data and the free movement of personal data within the European Union. The right to privacy is a highly developed area of law in Europe where privacy is viewed as a fundamental right of all individuals.

The EU Data Protection Directive states that personal data should not be processed unless certain conditions are met. These conditions fall into three categories: (1) transparency, (2) legitimate purpose, and (3) proportionality. Each member state must also set up a supervisory authority, an independent body that will (a) monitor the data protection level in that member state, (b) give advice to the government about administrative measures and regulations, and (c) start legal proceedings when the state's national data protection regulation has been violated.

In accordance with the EU Data Protection Directive, personal data may only be transferred to a country outside of the EU if that country provides an "adequate level of protection." Major countries that have been deemed adequate by the European Commission are Andorra, Argentina, Canada, Iceland, Israel, Liechtenstein, Switzerland, and Uruguay.

If a country has not been deemed adequate (for example, the United States), four options exist for transferring personal data out of the EU and to that country:

1. Model contracts have been drafted by the European Commission that when executed by an organization importing data from the EU ensure an adequate level of protection through contractual provisions in the model contracts.

2. Binding corporate rules ("BCRs") are internal rules (such as a Code of Conduct) adopted by a multinational group of related organizations which permit international transfers of personal data to related companies located in countries which do not provide an adequate level of protection. For example, if a German company has a subsidiary in the United States, and the company desires to transfer personal data to its subsidiary, it may establish BCRs with its subsidiary that, when approved by the German data protection authority, permit the transfer.

3. The U.S. Department of Commerce in consultation with the European Commission has developed a <u>Safe Harbor program</u> that permits the transfer of personal data out of the European Union to U.S. companies that have agreed to participate in the program.

4. The data subject may <u>unambiguously consent</u> to the transfer. Specifically, in accordance with the EU Data Protection Directive, the data subject may provide "any freely given specific and informed indication of his wishes" to have the data transferred.

Figure 5 illustrates the four ways an organization may legally transfer personal information outside of the EU to a country that has not been deemed to provide an adequate level of protection.

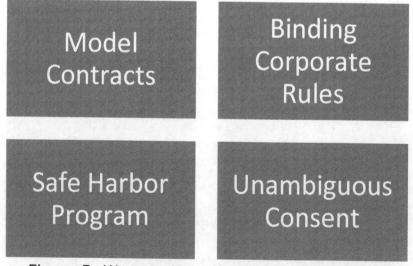

Figure 5: Ways to Transfer Data out of the EU

All member states of the EU are also signatories of the European Convention on Human Rights ("ECHR"). Article 8 of the ECHR provides that every individual has "the right to respect for his private and family life, his home and his correspondence," subject to certain restrictions. In particular, any interference with an individual's right of privacy must be in accordance with law and necessary in a democratic society, in view of such public interests as national security and the prevention of crime.

In addition to the European Union, other regional organizations have adopted major privacy initiatives. In 2004, for example, the Asia-Pacific Economic Cooperation ("APEC") adopted a privacy system that is a self-regulatory code of conduct designed to create more consistent privacy protection for consumers when their data moves between countries with different privacy regimes in the APEC region. The FTC and the U.S. Department of Commerce helped develop the APEC privacy rules. In addition to the United States, the other APEC members include Australia, Brunei, Canada, Chile, China, Hong Kong, Indonesia, Japan, Korea, Malaysia, Mexico, New Zealand, Papua New Guinea, Peru, the Philippines, Russia, Singapore, Taiwan, Thailand, and Vietnam.

In 2009, over 80 countries adopted and approved the "Madrid Resolution" on international privacy. The purpose of the Madrid Resolution was twofold: (1) define a set of principles and rights guaranteeing the effective and internationally uniform protection of privacy and (2) facilitate the international flow of personal data needed in a globalized world. In accordance with the Madrid Resolution, the data controller (referred to as the "responsible party") has a duty of confidentiality with respect to a data subject's personal data. In addition, the data controller must protect personal data with "appropriate technical and organizational measures to ensure ... their integrity, confidentiality and availability."

D. Federal Privacy Laws in the United States

For the Certification Foundation exam, you are expected to understand the basics of several United States laws that regulate the processing of personal information. As previously mentioned, the United States takes a sectoral approach to privacy protection, regulating specific industries with separate legislation.

Important federal laws regulating the private sector in the United States include (1) the Fair Credit Reporting Act ("FCRA"), (2) the Gramm-Leach-Bliley Act ("GLBA"), (3) the Health Insurance Portability and Accountability Act ("HIPAA"), and (4) the Children's Online Privacy Protection Act ("COPPA"). Important federal laws regulating the public sector include (1) the Privacy Act of 1974 and (2) the Freedom of Information Act ("FOIA"). Each of these federal laws is discussed more fully below.

1. U.S. Laws Regulating the Private Sector

Let's begin with the two private sector federal laws that regulate the financial industry. The Fair Credit Reporting Act ("FCRA") was originally enacted in 1970 and was updated by the Fair and Accurate Credit Transactions Act of 2003 ("FACTA"). The FCRA applies to (1) consumer reporting agencies (e.g., Experian, TransUnion, and Equifax) and (2) users of consumer reports. The purpose of the FCRA is to increase the accuracy and fairness of credit reporting and to limit the use of consumer reports to permissible purposes, such as for employment and the underwriting of insurance. The FCRA requires users of consumer reports to provide notice to the consumer, obtain consumer reports only for a permissible purpose, and provide certification of the user's permissible purpose to the credit reporting agency.

The Gramm-Leach-Bliley Act ("GLBA"), also known as the "Financial Services Modernization Act," was enacted in 1999. It applies to institutions that are significantly engaged in financial activities in the United States (also known as "domestic financial institutions"). The GLBA requires domestic financial institutions to, among other things, provide an initial privacy notice when the customer relationship is established (and annually thereafter) and provide an opt-out notice prior to sharing non-public personal information with unaffiliated third parties.
The next important federal law regulates the processing of personal information in the healthcare industry in the United States. The Health Insurance Portability and Accountability Act ("HIPAA") was enacted in 1996 to define policies, procedures, and guidelines that covered entities must adhere to for maintaining the privacy and security of individually identifiable protected health information ("PHI").

Covered entities generally include healthcare clearinghouses, employer sponsored health plans, health insurers, and health care providers. As directed by Title II of HIPAA, the Department of Health and Human Services ("HHS") has promulgated two important rules to address the handling of PHI: (1) the Privacy Rule and (2) the Security Rule.

Under the Privacy Rule, covered entities may disclose PHI to facilitate treatment, payment, or health care operations without a patient's express written authorization. Any other disclosure of PHI requires written authorization from the data subject for the disclosure. In addition, when a covered entity discloses PHI, it must make a reasonable effort to disclose only the <u>minimum necessary</u> information required to achieve its purpose.

While the Privacy Rule pertains to all forms of PHI, including paper and electronic records, the Security Rule deals specifically with electronic Protected Health Information ("ePHI"). In accordance with the Security Rule, covered entities must implement three types of security safeguards to protect ePHI:
(1) administrative, (2) physical, and (3) technical. For each of these types of safeguards, the Security Rule identifies various security standards, and for each standard it provides both required and addressable implementation specifications.

The final important private sector law regulating the processing of personal information is the Children's Online Privacy Protection Act ("COPPA"). COPPA was enacted in 1998 to curtail the collection of personal information from children. The Act applies to websites and online services operated for commercial purposes that are either directed to children under the age of 13 or have actual knowledge that children under the age of 13 are providing information online. In addition to requiring operators of these websites to conspicuously post a privacy notice, COPPA also requires that the website operator obtain verifiable parental consent prior to any collection, use, or disclosure of personal information from persons under the age of 13.

2. U.S. Laws Regulating the Public Sector

Now let's turn to the public sector laws. The Privacy Act of 1974 establishes fair information principles for the collection, maintenance, use, and dissemination of personally identifiable information that is maintained in systems operated by the federal government. The Privacy Act prohibits the disclosure of information from a federally operated system of records absent the written consent of the data subject. The Act also provides individuals with a means by which to seek access to their records and sets forth various agency record-keeping requirements.

The Freedom of Information Act ("FOIA") is a federal freedom of information law enacted in 1966 that allows for the full or partial disclosure of previously unreleased information and documents controlled by the United States government. FOIA defines agency records subject to disclosure, outlines mandatory disclosure procedures, and grants nine statutory exemptions to disclosure, such as federal records containing trade secrets.

Again, for the Certification Foundation exam, you are expected to understand only the basics of these federal laws. The second part of this guide, which focuses on the CIPP/US exam, elaborates on each of these laws.

Chapter 3: Internet Privacy

This chapter addresses privacy issues related to websites and other online activities. You should expect anywhere from 20 to 24 questions on your examination directed to subject matter from this chapter.

A. Glossary Terms

As previously mentioned, many questions on the exam will come directly from the definitions provided in the IAPP's glossary. Therefore, it is important that you read the definitions provided in the glossary for the terms listed below. The glossary is located at:

http://www.cippexam.com/glossary

Glossary Terms: Active Data Collection, Authentication, Behavioral Advertising, Caching, Children's Online Privacy Protection Act of 2000, Cookie, Cookie Directive, Cross-site Scripting, Cryptography, Customer Access, Encryption, Extensible Markup Language, Flash, Hyperlink, Hypertext Markup Language, Hypertext Transfer Protocol, Hypertext Transfer Protocol Secure, Internet Protocol Address, Internet Service Provider, JavaScript, Just-in-time Notification, Layered Notice, Location-based Service, Online Behavioral Advertising, Passive Data Collection, Phishing, Privacy by Design, Secure Sockets Layer, Social Engineering, SPAM, Stored Communications Act, Syndicated Content, Transmission Control Protocol, Transport Layer Security, Uniform Resource Locator, Web Beacon.

B. Overview of Internet Technologies

The Internet is a global system of interconnected computer networks that uses standard communications protocols to serve several billion users worldwide. It is a massive system that consists of millions of private, public, academic, business, and government networks that are linked together by a broad array of electronic, wireless, and optical networking technologies.

The two most ubiquitous web technologies are Hypertext Transfer Protocol ("HTTP") and Hypertext Markup Language ("HTML"). As its name suggests, HTTP is a protocol that facilitates the transfer of data on the Internet. Generally, an HTTP client sends a request message (e.g., a request for a webpage) to an HTTP server. The server, in turn, returns a response message (e.g., the requested webpage).

HTML is the main markup language for creating web pages and other information that can be displayed in a web browser. The language instructs a web browser how to render, or display, a webpage. A webpage written in HTML is accessed by an HTTP client through a unique Internet address called a uniform resource locator ("URL"). The URL is a specific character string that acts as a reference to online resource. For example, http://www.cippexam.com is an example of a URL for a webpage that offers this guide for sale.

A URL typically consists of a protocol identifier (e.g., "http") followed by a second-level domain (e.g., "cippexam") followed by a top-level domain (e.g., ".com"). Some URLs, as provided in the above example, include a sub-domain (e.g., "www").

Numerous other technologies are part of the Internet protocol suite. For example, transmission control protocol ("TCP") and Internet protocol ("IP") provide end-to-end connectivity for clients and servers. These two protocols specify how data should be formatted, addressed, transmitted, routed, and received on the Internet.

In addition, there are two important security protocols used to protect information, including personal information, on the Internet. Transport layer security ("TLS") and its predecessor, secure sockets layer ("SSL"), are cryptographic protocols that provide secure communications over the Internet. Several versions of TLS and SSL are widely used in popular Internet applications, such as web browsing, email, Internet faxing, instant messaging, and voice-over-IP ("VoIP").

C. Online Privacy Notices

Most organizations develop comprehensive privacy notices to communicate to the public the organization's information handling practices and policies. These privacy notices typically take the form of a detailed webpage accessible from the organization's homepage. A privacy notice should include (1) a description of the types of information collected, (2) any uses or disclosures of the information, (3) choices available to the website user (e.g., the ability to opt in or opt out of certain activities), (4) contact information for the organization, and (5) the effective date of the notice.

Privacy notices should also be regularly reviewed and any substantial changes communicated to the user.

For example, when information is shared or used in a way not currently addressed by the privacy notice, an organization should notify its users and update its privacy notice to describe the new use of the data.

The goals of a privacy notice are to create transparency in an organization's data collection practices and to help users make informed decisions. Unfortunately, most users do not read privacy notices because they are drafted in a verbose and legally formalistic manner.

Layered privacy notices address this concern by presenting the user with a short notice that is simple and concise. This short notice summarizes the organization's information handling practices and the choices available to users. The full privacy notice is typically accessible by a hyperlink from the short notice if the user wants more information about the organization's privacy practices. Thus, layered notices provide a quick and easy way for a user to understand an organization's information handling practices and the choices available to that user. As such, layered privacy notices are overwhelmingly preferred by Internet users. Privacy laws, however, do not mandate which form of notice must be provided. Therefore, companies are free to choose a layered privacy notice or a more traditional form.

D. Online Data Collection

Web forms are the most common mechanism for collecting personal information on the Internet. Web forms are a type of interface presented to a user of a website for inputting and transmitting data, including personal data.

The three main input elements used by web forms to collect data are (1) text boxes, (2) checkboxes, and (3) radio buttons. From an information security perspective, check boxes and radio button are preferred because a user's input is limited and confined. The user either checks the box or selects the button or leaves it unchecked or unselected. Text boxes, on the other hand, allow a user to enter data that may cause unexpected results when processed by an application. For example, a user may enter a large amount of data into a text box which may cause a buffer overflow in a web application that tries to process the data. Therefore, text boxes should only be used when necessary and limits should be placed on the size of the text box (that is, the number of characters allowed to be entered into the text box).

There are two primary ways that websites collect data from users: (1) active data collection, and (2) passive data collection. Active data collection occurs when a user deliberately enters information into a web form, or otherwise actively provides the information for processing.

Passive data collection, on the other hand, occurs when data is indirectly collected without any overt user interaction. Passive collection is generally used to capture user preferences and usage behavior, including location data from personal mobile devices. The most widely used example of passive data collection is the placement of web cookies on a user's computer to capture Internet browsing history.

E. Intrusions to Online Privacy

With billions of users on the Internet, there are bound to be some users with less than altruistic motives. Internet users face a numbers of intrusions to their privacy, some of which are illegal and others that are just annoying. Some of the more problematic intrusions are (1) spam, (2) malware, and (3) phishing.

Spam refers to unsolicited commercial email. Spam is also sometimes referred to as "bulk" commercial email because a large number of recipients typically receive the message. Spam can clog a user's mailbox, making him less productive and frustrated. Spam also often contains inappropriate content, such as an offer for sale of illegal prescription drugs or pirated software. Recently, spam accounted for more than 70% of all electronic messages, with more than 40 billion spam message sent each day.

Another abusive practice on the Internet is the distribution of malware. Malware, short for malicious software, is a computer program used or designed by attackers to disrupt a computer's operation, gather sensitive information, or gain access to a private computer system. Malware is a general term used to describe a variety of forms of intrusive software. Malware includes computer viruses, worms, Trojan horses, rootkits, keyloggers, spyware, adware, and other malicious programs.

Finally, phishing is the act of acquiring information, such as usernames, passwords, and credit card numbers, by masquerading as a trustworthy entity in an electronic communication. Electronic messages purporting to be from IT administrators, banks, and government agencies are commonly used to lure the unsuspecting receivers of these fraudulent communication. Phishing emails may also contain links to websites that are infected with malware.

One type of phishing, called "spear phishing," is a phishing attempt directed at a specific individual or company. With spear phishing, an attacker first gathers information about their often high-profile target to increase the probability of a successful attack. For example, an attacker may send an email to the chief financial officer ("CFO") of a company pretending to be the company's chief executive officer ("CEO"). In the message, the attacker may request that the CFO provide internal financial data by return message. Because the attacker has personalized the communication, the chances of the CFO actually sending the requested data are increased. This is an example of spear phishing, which is a personalized and targeted attack.

F. Online Behavioral Advertising

Online behavioral advertising (also known as "targeted advertising") refers to a range of technologies and techniques used by online advertisers to increase the effectiveness of their advertising campaigns by capturing data generated by website visitors. For example, a commercial website may track a user's browsing history and automatically serve advertisements for products related to the content previously viewed by the user. When targeted advertising is done without the knowledge of the user, it may be a breach of browser security and potentially even illegal.

In 2010, the Federal Trade Commission proposed a new regulatory framework for consumer data privacy, including a proposal for a "Do Not Track" mechanism which would allow Internet users to opt out of online behavioral advertising. The FTC stated, "[t]he most practical method of providing uniform choice for online behavioral advertising would likely involve placing a setting similar to a persistent cookie on a consumer's browser and conveying that setting to sites that the browser visits, to signal whether or not the consumer wants to be tracked or receive targeted advertisements."

Web cookies (also known as "HTTP cookies" or "browser cookies") are frequently used for online behavioral advertising. A web cookie is a small piece of data sent from a website and stored in a user's web browser. Every time the user loads the website, the browser sends the cookie back to the server to notify the website of the user's presence and previous activity. Web cookies were designed to reliably retain state information (such as items in a shopping cart) and to record the user's browsing activity, including clicking particular buttons, logging in, or recording which pages were visited by the user.

Web cookies are classified as either first-party or third-party cookies. First-party cookies are cookies that belong to the same domain as the webpage that a user is currently viewing (as indicated in the browser's address bar). Third-party cookies, on the other hand, are cookies that belong to domains different from the one shown in the address bar. For example, if you are viewing the website http://www.amazon.com, first-party cookies are those cookies from Amazon. Third-party cookies would be those cookies from all other domains, such as doubleclick.net, a popular advertising website. Web pages can feature content from third-party domains (such as banner advertisements), which opens up the potential for tracking the user's browsing history. Privacy setting options in most modern browsers allow a user to block third-party cookies because of privacy concerns.

Web cookies are further classified as either session or persistent cookies. A session cookie (also known as an "in-memory cookie" or "transient cookie") exists in temporary memory only while the user is reading and navigating the website. Web browsers delete session cookies when the user closes the browser or restarts his computer.

On the other hand, a persistent cookie is written to disk and stored until the expiration date contained in the cookie. For example, if a persistent cookie has its expiration date set to 1 year, then within the year, the data in the cookie would be sent back to the server every time the user visited the server. The cookie would automatically expire upon the 1 year expiration date and be deleted from the user's computer.

A persistent cookie may be used to record a vital piece of information, such as a user's login credentials. For this reason, persistent cookies are also called "tracking cookies." Persistent cookies enable the "remember me" functionality found on most websites that automatically logs a user back into the website.

In the EU, the E-Privacy Directive of 2009 (also known as the "Cookie Directive") recognizes the importance and usefulness of cookies for the functioning of the modern Internet but also warns of the danger that cookies may present to privacy. Specifically, the

Directive requires that a user provide affirmative consent before a cookie is stored on the user's computer. Therefore, much of Europe has adopted an opt-in approach to persistent web cookies, thereby requiring a user's informed consent before cookies can be stored on the user's computer.

G. Recent Developments in Online Privacy

The section addresses two recent issues related to online privacy: (1) cloud computing and (2) mobile computing. Both topics are frequently tested on the Certification Foundation exam, and therefore you should carefully read this section.

1. Cloud Computing

Cloud computing is a colloquial expression used to describe a variety of different types of computing concepts that involve a large number of computers connected through a real-time communications network (typically, the Internet). Cloud computing relies on the sharing of resources to achieve coherence and economies of scale similar to a utility (such as an electricity grid) but over a computer network. The five main characteristics of cloud computing are (1) on-demand self-service, (2) broad network access, (3) resource pooling, (4) rapid elasticity, and (5) measured service. Each of these characteristics is shown in Figure 6 on the following page.

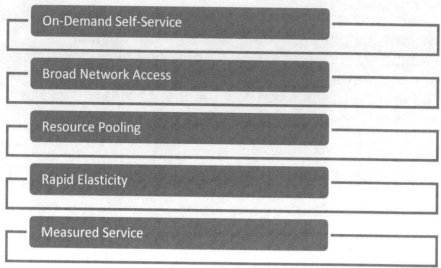

Figure 6: Characteristics of Cloud Computing

In addition to the five characteristics of cloud computing, there are three main service models of cloud computing: (1) Infrastructure as a Service ("IaaS"), (2) Platform as a Service ("PaaS"), and (3) Software as a service ("SaaS"). IaaS is the most basic cloud service model. In IaaS, users rent computing resources, such as storage, network capacity, and processing power from a cloud provider. The cloud provider owns the equipment and is responsible for housing, running, and maintaining it.

Under PaaS, a cloud provider delivers a computing platform, typically including an operating system, database, and web server. Web developers build and publish web applications using the platform.

Finally, SaaS is a software delivery model in which applications and associated data are centrally hosted in the cloud. Customers typically access the applications through a web browser over the Internet. SaaS is often referred to as "on-demand software."

Cloud computing may also be classified according to its deployment model. Four main types of clouds exist: (1) private clouds, (2) public clouds, (3) community clouds, and (4) hybrid clouds.

A private cloud is operated solely for a single organization, whether managed, hosted internally, or hosted externally. Conversely, a public cloud is offered to the general public through the Internet. Thus, public clouds are generally less secure than private clouds.

Community clouds are collaborative efforts in which infrastructure is shared between several organizations from a specific community. For example, several auction websites, such as eBay, may decide to join a community cloud for hosting their similar sites.

Finally, a hybrid cloud is a composition of at least one private cloud and at least one public cloud. A hybrid cloud is typically offered in one of two ways: a vendor has a private cloud and forms a partnership with a public cloud provider, or a public cloud provider forms a partnership with a vendor that provides private cloud platforms. In either case, the hybrid cloud offers both private and public computing platforms.

2. Mobile Computing

Mobile computing devices are everywhere today. Most individuals in industrialized countries either carry a mobile computing device (e.g., a smart phone, laptop, or tablet) or may be readily associated with a mobile computing device, such as an automobile's entertainment and navigational hub that is connected to the Internet. The ubiquity of mobile computing devices has created new concerns for privacy practitioners. Chief among these concerns is how mobile devices store, distribute, and secure location data. Because of its ability to uniquely identify an individual, location information is considered personal information in many jurisdictions, and it is entitled to the same protections as all other types of personal information in these jurisdictions.

Today, mobile devices can determine and distribute a user's location using the global positioning system ("GPS") and other techniques in real-time. Consequently, location has become a new data element that has both privacy and security implications. Advertisers can target users based on their location (e.g., send an advertisement for a cold beverage in areas where the temperature is hot), criminals may target unsuspecting visitors to new cities, and the government could use location information to track a foreigner's movements. All of these situations highlight why location data is an often-debated subject for privacy practitioners. When using mobile computing devices, it is important to acknowledge and address the privacy issues associated with location information.

Chapter 4: Information Security

This chapter addresses procedures and techniques for securing information in both electronic and paper form. You should expect anywhere from 12 to 14 questions on your examination directed to subject matter from this chapter.

A. Glossary Terms

Many questions on the exam come from definitions provided in the IAPP's glossary. Therefore, you should read the definitions provided in the glossary for the important terms listed below. The glossary is located at:

http://www.cippexam.com/glossary

Glossary Terms: Application-Layer Attacks, Authentication, Authorization, Biometrics, Breach Disclosure, Cloud Computing, Computer Forensics, Confidentiality, Cryptography, Data Breach, Encryption, Extranet, Information Privacy, Information Security, Internet Protocol Address, Internet Service Provider, Intrusion Detection System, Intrusion Prevention System, ISO 27002, Least Privilege, Local Area Network, Logs, Multi-factor Authentication, Network-Layer Attacks, Non-repudiation, Perimeter Controls, Privacy by Design, Public-key Infrastructure, Risk Assessment Factors, Role-based Access Controls, Secret Key, Trojan Horse, Virtual Private Network, Voice Over Internet Protocol, Wide Area Network.

B. Overview of Information Security Fundamentals

Information security is the practice of protecting information from unauthorized access, use, disclosure, disruption, or modification. The most well-known model for information security is called the "C-I-A triad," referring to Confidentiality, Integrity, and Availability, as depicted below.

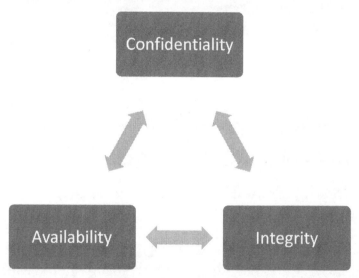

Figure 7: Information Security Model

The C-I-A model is a global framework and is reflected in numerous information privacy laws across the world. For example, in accordance with the 2009 Madrid Resolution, a data controller must protect personal data with appropriate safeguards to ensure its "integrity, confidentiality and availability."

With respect to the C-I-A model, confidentiality refers to preventing disclosure of information to unauthorized individuals or systems. Integrity refers to maintaining and assuring the accuracy and consistency of information over its entire lifecycle.

Finally, availability refers to the ability of authorized users to access information.

Organizations implement information security by creating one or more controls or safeguards that mitigate the risk to the information. As previously addressed in Chapter 1, these safeguards are generally classified into three groups:
(1) administrative, (2) physical, and (3) technical.

C. Information Security Policies

An information security policy is an internal statement that an organization adopts to describe the procedures in place that protect its informational assets. An information security policy should address (1) the restrictions placed on an information technology system, such as password polices and access control mechanisms, and (2) the users of the system, who may be employees of the organizations or outside vendors assisting the organization.

The International Organization for Standardization ("ISO") has developed standards related to information security. For example, ISO 27001 specifies a management system that is intended to bring information security under explicit management control. ISO 27001 requires that management (1) systematically examine the organization's information security risks, (2) design and implement a coherent and comprehensive suite of information security controls to address risks that are deemed unacceptable, and (3) adopt an overarching management process to ensure that the information security controls meet the organization's information security needs on an ongoing basis.

ISO 27002 is an information security standard that provides best practices for information security professionals. The standard defines information security within the context of the C-I-A triad: "the preservation of confidentiality (ensuring that information is accessible only to those authorized to have access), integrity (safeguarding the accuracy and completeness of information and processing methods), and availability (ensuring that authorized users have access to information and associated assets when required)." Organizations can use ISO 27001 and 27002 as a framework for an effective information security program.

D. Information Classification

When creating an information security policy, it is important to recognize that not all information should be treated equally. Confidential and sensitive information demands greater protection. Conversely, publicly available and well-known information typically requires less protection. An organization's information should be classified into several groups (depending upon its importance and sensitivity), and the appropriate controls should be placed around access to these groups of information.

The most common information classification scheme divides information into three categories:

1. Public: information by its very nature is designed to be shared broadly, without restriction. Examples include marketing material, press releases, and regulatory reports submitted to government agencies.

2. <u>Sensitive</u>: information that is considered internal and should not be released outside of the organization. Examples include business plans, financial data, and documents reflecting corporate strategy.

3. <u>Confidential</u>: information that is generally intended for a very specific purpose and should not be disclosed to anyone without a demonstrated need to know. Examples include employee bank account information, Social Security numbers, and login credentials (e.g., username and password).

Typically, very few controls should be placed on public information. Controls suitable for public information include mechanisms that prevent unauthorized modification or alteration. For example, although a corporate press release is generally public information, an organization should prevent unauthorized individuals from altering the press release and thereby potentially disseminating incorrect or fraudulent information. Access to public information is generally not restricted.

For sensitive information, safeguards should prevent unauthorized modification or alteration and control access to the sensitive information. For example, sensitive information may be encrypted or password protected. In additional, logs may be used to record who accessed or modified the sensitive information.

With respect to confidential information, additional controls should be implemented above and beyond the controls already in place for sensitive information. These additional controls may include having individuals with access to the confidential information execute non-disclosure agreements and storing confidential information on a separate and secure data server.

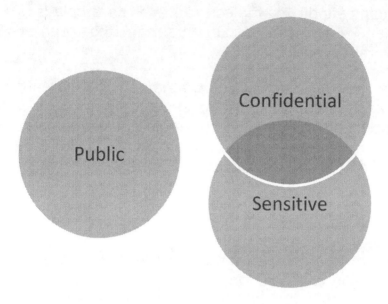

Figure 8: Information Classifications

As shown in Figure 8, certain types of information may be both confidential and sensitive. Public information, however, generally cannot be confidential or sensitive because public information by its nature is already widely known.

E. Information Risk Assessment

Risk can be broadly defined as the likelihood of an undesirable event occurring after taking into account any controls in place to mitigate the undesirable event. An industry accepted formulation of information technology risk is:

$$Risk = \sum_{i=1}^{n} Threat_i * Vulnerability_i * Expected\ Loss_i$$

As indicated by the above formula, the total risk associated with an organization's information technology is directly related to three parameters: (1) threats, (2) vulnerabilities, and (3) expected loss.

Threats are any circumstances that may cause an undesirable event to an organization's information, such as a data breach or fire. Vulnerabilities are weaknesses in an organization's information systems, policies, or procedures. When a threat exploits some vulnerability, a security event that creates risk occurs. The amount of the risk for a particular security event is equal to the probability of the event occurring times the expected loss associated with the event. Summing the risks associated with all security events at an organization results in the total information risk.

The Certification Foundation exam typically contains several questions related to the formulation of risk. Therefore, you should know the basic formula and the three components used to calculate risk.

F. Technical Controls for Information Security

Technical controls are safeguards or countermeasures that help an organization avoid, counteract, or minimize security risks relating to information stored in an information technology system. Remember, these technical controls are just one of the three main types of controls (the other two being administrative controls and physical controls).

Technical security controls can be classified into the following three primary types:

1. Preventive: controls designed to protect information before a security event occurs. Examples include firewalls, passwords, and encryption.

2. Detective: controls designed to protect information during a security event. Examples include security logs and intrusion detection systems.

3. Corrective: controls designed to protect information after a security event occurs. Examples include intrusion preventive systems that automatically block or limit users with suspicious activity.

More than one type of control may be used to protect information. For example, confidential information should be protected by several controls of varying classes. Information of lower importance, such as public information, may be protected by fewer controls, or even no controls if the cost of implementing the controls outweighs their anticipated benefits.

Determining who at an organization has access to particular types of information is an important process that an organization must undertake when developing its security policy. As a general matter, employees should only be given access to information that is needed for them to fulfill their job responsibilities. No greater access should be provided. Role-based access controls are routinely used to restrict access to authorized roles and users at an organization.

G. Basic Principles of Information Security

When implementing security controls at an organization, it is important to keep in mind the two important principles of information security.

The first principle is called <u>separation of duties</u>. Separation of duties occurs when more than one person is required to complete a business task. For example, before paying an invoice, an employee may need to submit an expense report. After submitting the expense report, it may be routed to a manager for approval before being paid. By separating the ability to pay invoices into two requisite parts (that is, expense report generation and approval), an organization may deter fraud and reduce errors. This is a commonly employed example of the principle of separation of powers.

The second important principle of information security is called the <u>rule of least privilege</u>. In accordance with this rule, a user should only be provided the minimum access needed to accomplish a legitimate business task. The rule of least privilege limits the damage that can be caused by a rogue employee by limiting the level of access given to the employee. Role-based access controls are a common way to implement the rule of least privilege. With role-based access, all users are classified into one of several defined roles. For example, the system administrator may create a first role for employees who merely enter data into the system. A second role may be created for employees who audit or edit the data. Finally, a third role may be created for managers who approve the data. Various levels of access are assigned to each role depending on the functionality required to perform the responsibilities assigned to a specific role.

Some information technology departments grant more access than needed in order to minimize the number of support calls related to user access requests. For example, a new employee may be given the right to install new applications onto the employee's computer system even though all applications needed for the employee's job have already been preinstalled onto the computer. Although this may be a convenient solution for the information technology department, it presents a major threat to the security of an organization's data assets. Information security should be a well thought out plan with various predefined roles determining the amount of access provided to any particular user.

H. Incident Management and Response

Despite an organization's best efforts, security breaches will inevitably occur. When an incident occurs, an organization must know how to appropriately respond. As shown in Figure 9 on the following page, the basic incident management and response process includes: (1) incident discovery, (2) containment and analysis, (3) notification, and (4) eradication and future prevention.

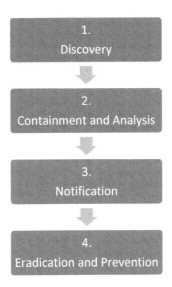

Figure 9: Incident Management Framework

The first step to incident management is discovery of the breach. After a breach is discovered, the breach should be contained by, for example, disabling affected user accounts. The containment process necessarily involves analysis of the breach to determine how it occurred. Notification is the third step when responding to a security breach. When and who to notify will depend on an organization's information security and privacy policies, as well as any applicable laws and regulations. In some cases, no notification may be required (for example, when the breach was limited to just public, non-personal information). The final step is eradication and prevention. Once it is known how the incident occurred, appropriate remedial steps should be taken as soon as possible to prevent any future harm. Eradication involves the removal of the threat and vulnerability that enabled the breach, while prevention relates to the actions that will preclude a similar breach from occurring in the future.

The incident management process described above provides an organization with a framework for dealing with and responding to information security breaches. Various additional steps may be added depending upon then size of an organization and the regulatory environment within which the organization operates.

Conclusion for the Certification Foundation Exam

Congratulations! You have completed the condensed text portion of this study guide for the Certification Foundation examination. The information you have just read was designed to provide you with the fundamentals of information privacy, and introduce you to the concepts that will be tested on the Certification Foundation exam. If you are new to information privacy, we recommend that you read the text a second time to ensure that you have fully absorbed and understand the material.

The next section of this guide contains sample questions with detailed answers. The questions are designed to supplement the material contained in the text portion of the guide. Therefore, do not worry if some of the concepts are new to you. The sample questions are designed to teach you new material and not to simply test your ability to remember the material presented in the beginning of this guide.

The questions below test facts that may appear on your exam. Thus, it is important that you carefully read both the questions and detailed answers provided. You will likely receive dozens of questions on your examination that test similar facts as our sample questions. If you answer these questions correctly, you are well on your way to passing the Certification Foundation examination and becoming a certified privacy professional.

Sample Questions for the Certification Foundation Exam

1. Which of the following may be classified as an unfair trade practice by the FTC?

   A. A website's privacy notice clearly states that it will not encrypt sensitive personal information, and the website operator does not, in fact, encrypt the data

   B. An organization promises to honor opt-out requests within 10 days but fails to honor opt-out requests within the stated timeframe

   C. A rogue employee steals credit card information even though the organization took reasonable precautions to protect the credit card information

   D. A federally insured bank does not comply with a regulation prohibiting the bank from revealing information about its customers

ANSWER: A. Section 5 of the FTC Act prohibits "unfair or deceptive acts or practices in or affecting commerce." Answer A is an example of an unfair trade practice because the website operator is not being deceptive, but the potential harm caused by the website operator's failure to encrypt sensitive data clearly outweighs the cost of providing encryption, a commonplace and inexpensive security control. Answer B is an example of a deceptive trade practice. When companies state that they will safeguard personal information, the FTC can and does take law enforcement action to make sure that companies live up to these promises. A violation of a promise made in a privacy notice is an example of a deceptive trade practice. Answer C is not an unfair trade practice because the organization has implemented reasonable security measures, and the employee simply committed a crime, which is generally considered an unforeseeable event. Answer D is incorrect because the FTC has no jurisdiction over banks and common carriers, which are under the supervision of other governmental agencies.

2. In which service model of cloud computing are applications hosted by the cloud provider in the cloud and typically accessed by users through a web browser?

    A.   Infrastructure as a service ("IaaS")
    B.   Platform as a service ("PaaS")
    C.   Software as a service ("SaaS")
    D.   Network as a service ("NaaS")

ANSWER: C. With SaaS, applications are hosted by the cloud provider in the cloud. Customers typically access the applications through a web browser over the Internet. SaaS is often referred to as "on-demand software." IaaS is the most basic cloud service model. In IaaS, users rent computing resources, such as storage, network capacity, and processing power from cloud providers. The cloud provider owns the equipment and is responsible for housing, running, and maintaining it. Under PaaS, cloud providers deliver a computing platform, typically including an operating system, database, and web server. Web developers build and publish web applications using the platform.

3. Which of the following is NOT a principle set forth in the Guidelines on the Protection of Privacy and Transborder Flows of Personal Data adopted by the Organization for Economic Cooperation and Development in 1980 ("OECD Guidelines")?

   A.   Collection Limitation
   B.   Openness
   C.   Mutual Consent
   D.   Security Safeguards

ANSWER: C. The eight principles contained in the OECD guidelines are: (1) collection limitation principles, (2) data quality principle, (3) purpose specification principle, (4) use limitation principle, (5) security safeguards principle, (6) openness principle, (7) individual participation principle, and (8) accountability principle. Mutual consent is not one of the principles in the OECD guidelines.

4. In which country is a person's tax return considered a public record?

   A.   Canada
   B.   Norway
   C.   China
   D.   Argentina

ANSWER: B. In Norway, tax returns are considered public records. Included within the tax return is a person's salary. Therefore, in Norway a person's salary is also a matter of public record. Finland and Sweden also treat tax returns as public records.

5. Which country takes a co-regulatory approach to privacy protection?

A. Israel
B. Canada
C. Zimbabwe
D. Morocco

ANSWER: B. Canada, Australia, and New Zealand are three countries employing a co-regulatory model of privacy protection.

6. Which of the following is an industry-accepted formula for assessing information security risk?

A. Risk = Threat x Vulnerability x Expected Loss
B. Risk = Control - Threat / Vulnerability
C. Risk = Threat + Vulnerability - Expected Loss
D. Risk = Threat x Vulnerability / Control

ANSWER: A. As indicated by the correct formula, information security risk is directly related to three parameters: (1) threats, (2) vulnerabilities, and (3) expected loss. A threat is any circumstance that may cause an undesirable event, such as a data breach. A vulnerability is a weaknesses in an organization's information systems, policies, or procedures. When a threat exploits some vulnerability, a security event that creates risk occurs. The amount of risk for a particular security event is equal to the probability of the event occurring times the expected loss associated with the event. Answers B – D set forth incorrect formulations of information security risk.

7. Information security policies and procedures should be communicated to which employees of an organization?

   A. All employees
   B. Employees in the information security department
   C. Managers
   D. The chief executive officer

ANSWER: A. All employees should be trained in information security best practices, and information security policies should be communicated to all employees, regardless of level. Even the lowest level employee can cause a security incident.

8. Which of the following is NOT generally performed by information security personnel at an organization?

   A. Enforce compliance with the information security policy
   B. Communicate the information security policy to employees
   C. Monitor for security incidents
   D. Develop an overall corporate security strategy

ANSWER: D. While information security personnel can perform a wide range of tasks related to information security at an organization, generally an executive, such as the chief security officer, will develop the corporate security policy.

9. What is the name of the backward looking process used to analyze how effectively an information security program has operated in the past?

A. Monitoring
B. Observation
C. Assessment
D. Planning

ANSWER: C. An assessment is the process used to evaluate how effectively an information security program has operated in the past. It generally includes an inventory all of data assets stored at an organization and the systems responsible for processing the data assets. Monitoring, observation, and planning are generally contemporaneous, or forward looking, processes.

10. Which one of the following is NOT a primary purpose of the APEC Privacy Framework, which was approved by the APEC ministers in 2004?

A. Improve information sharing among government agencies and regulators
B. Facilitate the safe transfer of information between economies
C. Encourage the use of electronic data as a means to enhance and expand business
D. Protect individuals from illegal data sharing practices

ANSWER: D. The Asia-Pacific Economic Cooperation ("APEC") Privacy Framework, which is consistent with the OECD's 1980 Guidelines, has the following primary goals: (1) improve information sharing among government agencies and regulators, (2) facilitate the safe transfer of information between economies, (3) establish a common set of privacy principles, (4) encourage the use of electronic data as a means to enhance and expand business, and (5) provide technical assistance to those economies that have yet to address privacy from a regulatory or policy perspective. Protecting individuals from illegal data sharing is not a primary purpose of the APEC Privacy Framework.

11.   Which of the following is typically the final step when establishing an information security program?

   A.   Monitor and review compliance with the security program
   B.   Identify and evaluate risks
   C.   Define the security policy
   D.   Review complaints and evaluations

ANSWER: A. Generally, an information security program should be established by (1) defining the security policy and security management system; (2) identifying and evaluating any risks, (3) selecting appropriate controls to address the identified risks, (4) obtaining management approval of program, and (5) monitoring and reviewing compliance with the program. Therefore, monitoring and reviewing compliance with the security program is the final step of the process.

12. Employee training on information security best practices is what type of security control?

A. Physical control
B. Administrative control
C. Technical control
D. Third-party control

ANSWER: B. Administrative controls are administrative actions, policies, and procedures that protect information. Employee training and incident response plans are types of administrative controls. Password authentication and firewalls are types of technical controls, while locks are examples of physical controls.

13. Effective information security considers what three central factors?

A. Confidentiality, integrity, and availability
B. Accountability, integrity, and autonomy
C. Confidentiality, integrity, and autonomy
D. Redundancy, reliability, and availability

ANSWER: A. The most well-known model for information security is called the C-I-A triad, referring to Confidentiality, Integrity, and Availability. Confidentiality refers to preventing the disclosure of information to unauthorized individuals or systems. Integrity refers to maintaining and assuring the accuracy and consistency of information over its entire lifecycle. Lastly, availability refers to the ability of authorized users to access the information. The C-I-A model is a global framework and is reflected in numerous information privacy laws across the world.

14. The National Do Not Call Registry is primarily enforced by which entities?

    A. Department of Transportation and FTC
    B. U.S. Department of Justice and FTC
    C. Department of Commerce and FCC
    D. FTC and FCC

ANSWER: D. Pursuant to its authority under the Telephone Consumer Protection Act ("TCPA"), the Federal Communication Commission ("FCC") established, together with the Federal Trade Commission ("FTC"), a national Do Not Call Registry in 2003. The registry is nationwide in scope, applies to all telemarketers (with the exception of certain non-profit organizations), and covers both interstate and intrastate telemarketing calls. Commercial telemarketers are not allowed to call you if your number is on the registry, subject to certain exceptions. The FTC and FCC are the primary enforcers of the National Do Not Call Registry.

15. Which country released a report in February of 2011 that provides guidance for utility companies on building smart grids with "privacy by design" principles?

    A. United Stated
    B. Canada
    C. Germany
    D. Australia

ANSWER: B. The Information and Privacy Commissioner of Ontario, Canada developed the "privacy by design" framework in the 1990s. It includes the following seven principles: (1) Proactive not Reactive; Preventative not Remedial; (2) Privacy as the Default Setting; (3) Privacy Embedded into Design, (4) Full Functionality — Positive-Sum, not Zero-Sum; (5) End-to-End Security — Full Lifecycle Protection; (6)Visibility and Transparency — Keep it Open; and (7) Respect for User Privacy — Keep it User-Centric. In February 2011, the Information and Privacy Commissioner released a report titled "Operationalizing Privacy by Design: The Ontario Smart Grid Case Study." The report provides guidance for utility companies on building smart grids with privacy by design principles.

16. When do confidentiality and privacy issues exist with respect to human resources information?

   A. During the candidate screening and interview process
   B. During employment
   C. After an employee is terminated or discharged
   D. All of the above

ANSWER: D. Confidentiality and privacy issues exist whenever an organization is holding personal information concerning its prospective, current, or former employees. Therefore, privacy issues exist before, during, and after employment, including (1) at the screening and interview stage, (2) during employment, and (3) after termination.

17. Which of the following accurately describes the EU Data Protection Directive?

A. It applies to personal information held by the private sector and not the government
B. There are typically less strict legal rules for government organizations that hold personal information than for private organizations
C. Sensitive information is referred to as "protected classes of data"
D. Business contact information is classified as sensitive information

ANSWER: B. Although the EU Data Protection Directive applies to both the public and private sectors, less strict legal rules generally apply to government agencies than to private organizations. For example, the processing of personal information may occur without consent if the processing is necessary to perform tasks related to the public interest or tasks carried out by official authorities. The EU Data Protection Directive uses the term "special categories of data" to describe sensitive personal information (not "protected classes data"). In accordance with the Directive, special categories of data include personal data revealing racial or ethnic origin, political opinions, religious or philosophical beliefs, trade-union membership, and the processing of data concerning health or sex life. Business contact information is not classified as sensitive information.

18.   Wiretap laws primarily protect what type of information?

   A.   The identity of the sender and receiver of communications
   B.   The location of the sender and receiver of communications
   C.   The content of communications
   D.   The date and time of communications

ANSWER: C. Wiretapping is the monitoring of telephone and Internet conversations by a third party, often through covert means. Wiretap laws primarily protect the content of communications. While wiretaps can reveal the identity and location of the sender and receiver, as well as the date and time of a communication, these facts are all secondary types of information that may be protected when disclosed by the content of the communication. Therefore, C is the correct answer.

19. Which of the following is NOT a major reason why health information is considered sensitive in most jurisdictions?

   A. Drug companies may market new and untested drugs to individuals with ailments if health information is not protected as sensitive information
   B. Patients are forthcoming with their doctors when health information is protected as sensitive information
   C. Employers may treat employees unequally and potentially discriminate against employees if health information is not classified as sensitive information
   D. Health information is inherently private and sensitive because it relates to the inner workings of a person's mind and body

ANSWER: A. Answers B, C, and D present the three major reasons why countries classify health information as sensitive information. The possibility of drug companies marketing untested drugs to consumers is not a major reason why health information is classified as sensitive personal information.

20. Which Middle East country requires that databases storing sensitive personal information be registered with the government?

   A. Iran
   B. Israel
   C. Egypt
   D. Jordan

ANSWER: B. Israel's Protection of Privacy law requires registration of any database that includes sensitive information. More specifically, it requires registration of a database if (1) the database includes information about more than 10,000 persons; (2) the database includes sensitive information; (3) the database includes information about persons and the information was not provided to the database by them, on their behalf, or with their consent; (4) the database belongs to a public body; or (5) the database is used for direct mail.

21. Which Latin American country was one of the first countries deemed by the EU Commission as providing an adequate level of protection?

A. Argentina
B. Chile
C. Columbia
D. Uruguay

ANSWER: A. In 2003, Argentina became the first Latin American country deemed by the EU Commission as providing an adequate level of protection. Argentina was also the first Latin American country to enact an omnibus data protection and privacy law. The EU Commission deemed Uruguay adequate in 2012. Chile and Columbia have not yet been deemed as providing an adequate level of protection.

22.   The federal Freedom of Information Act ("FOIA") covers which type of records?

A.   Executive branch records
B.   Congressional records
C.   Judicial records
D.   Records more than 10 years old

ANSWER: A. FOIA is a federal freedom of information law enacted in 1966, which allows for the full or partial disclosure of previously unreleased information and documents controlled by the United States government. FOIA explicitly applies only to executive branch government agencies, and therefore it does not apply to legislative and judicial branch records. FOIA defines agency records subject to disclosure, outlines mandatory disclosure procedures, and grants nine statutory exemptions to disclosure, such as records containing trade secrets.

23.   When a website operator states in its privacy notice that it will not share financial information with third parties and then shares financial information with a third-party affiliate, what recourse may occur?

A.   The FTC may bring an action for unfair competition against the operator
B.   The FTC may bring an action for a deceptive trade practice against the operator
C.   A user of the website may bring a criminal complaint against the operator
D.   The FTC may bring an action under Section 7 of the FTC Act

ANSWER: B. If an organization fails to comply with its privacy notice, it may be held liable by the FTC for a deceptive trade practice under Section 5 of the FTC Act, which prohibits "unfair or deceptive acts or practices in or affecting commerce." When companies state that they will safeguard personal information, the FTC can and does take law enforcement action to make sure that companies live up to these promises. A violation of a promise made in a privacy notice is an example of a deceptive trade practice. The distinction between a deceptive trade practice and an unfair trade practice is often tested on the exam.

24.   The Children's Online Privacy Protection Act ("COPPA") applies to whom?

    A.   Operators of websites soliciting business in the United States
    B.   Operators of websites soliciting financial information from customers in the United States
    C.   Operators of commercial websites that are directed to children under 13 years of age
    D.   Operators of commercial websites that are directed to children under 18 years of age

ANSWER: C. COPPA was enacted in 1998 to curtail the collection of personal information from children. The Act applies to websites and online services operated for commercial purposes that are either directed to children under the age of 13 or have actual knowledge that children under 13 are providing information online. In addition to requiring operators of these websites to conspicuously post a privacy notice, COPPA also requires that the website operator obtain verifiable parental consent prior to any collection, use, or disclosure of personal information from persons under the age of 13.

25. The Gramm-Leach-Bliley Act ("GLBA") applies to which organizations?

A. All organizations that process financial data
B. Financial organizations with more than 10,000 customers
C. All organizations regulated by the Department of Commerce
D. Domestic financial institutions

ANSWER: D. The GLBA, also known as the "Financial Services Modernization Act," was enacted in 1999. It applies to institutions that are significantly engaged in financial activities in the United States (also known as "domestic financial institutions"). The GLBA requires domestic financial institutions to, among other things, provide an initial privacy notice when the customer relationship is established (and annually thereafter) and provide opt-out notice prior to sharing non-public personal information with non-affiliated third parties.

26. What is the main purpose of the Fair Credit Reporting Act ("FCRA")?

A. Enable data reporters to efficiently report valid debts on a consumer's credit report

B. Allow employers to quickly access financial data of their employees

C. Increase the ability of the government to access consumer reports of suspected criminals

D. Increase the accuracy and fairness of credit reporting and to limit the use of consumer reports to permissible purposes

ANSWER: D. The FCRA was originally enacted in 1970 and was more recently updated by the Fair and Accurate Credit Transactions Act of 2003 ("FACTA"). The FCRA applies to consumer reporting agencies ("CRAs"), such as Experian, TransUnion, and Equifax, and to users of consumer reports. The purpose of the FCRA was to increase the accuracy and fairness of credit reporting and to limit the use of consumer reports to permissible purposes, such as for employment purposes and the underwriting of insurance.

27. What is the basic rule for processing protected health information under the Health Insurance Portability and Accountability Act ("HIPAA")?

   A. Patients must opt-in before their protected health information is shared with other organizations unless the purpose is for treatment, payment, or healthcare operations

   B. Patients must opt-out before their protected health information is shared with other organizations unless the purpose is for treatment, payment, or healthcare operations

   C. Processing of protected health information is prohibited for all purposes without opt-in consent

   D. Processing of protected health information is prohibited for all purposes without opt-out consent

ANSWER: A. Under HIPAA's Privacy Rule, covered entities may disclose protected heath information ("PHI") to facilitate treatment, payment, or healthcare operations without a patient's express written authorization. Any other disclosure of PHI requires the covered entity to obtain written authorization from the data subject for the disclosure (that is, opt-in consent). In addition, when a covered entity discloses PHI, it must also make reasonable efforts to disclose only the minimum necessary information required to achieve its purpose.

28. In accordance with the Health Insurance Portability and Accountability Act ("HIPAA"), the Department of Health and Human Services ("HHS") has promulgated which of the following rules to address the handling of protected health information?

A. Transaction Rule and Equal Access Rule
B. Privacy Rule and the Security Rule
C. Privacy Rule and Equal Access Rule
D. Security Rule and the Notification Rule

ANSWER: B. The Health Insurance Portability and Accountability Act (HIPAA) was enacted in 1996 to define policies, procedures, and guidelines that covered entities must adhere to for maintaining the privacy and security of individually identifiable protected health information ("PHI"). Covered entities generally include healthcare clearinghouses, employer sponsored health plans, health insurers, and healthcare providers. As directed by Title II of HIPAA, the Department of Health and Human Services ("HHS") has promulgated two important rules to address the handling of PHI: (1) the Privacy Rule and (2) the Security Rule.

29.   Which of the following is NOT a privacy principle of the Safe Harbor program developed by the Department of Commerce in consultation with the European Commission?

A.   Notice
B.   Onward transfer to third parties
C.   Equal Opportunity
D.   Security

ANSWER: C. The European Union ("EU") Data Protection Directive prohibits the transfer of personal data to non-EU countries that do not meet the EU's "adequacy" standard for privacy protection. While the United States and the EU share the goal of enhancing privacy protection for their citizens, the United States takes a different approach to privacy than that of the EU. The U.S. Department of Commerce in consultation with the European Commission developed the Safe Harbor framework to bridge these differences in approach and provide a streamlined means for U.S. organizations to comply with the EU's Data Protection Directive. Organizations desiring to join the program must comply with the seven Safe Harbor privacy principles, which are: (1) notice, (2) choice, (3) onward transfer to third parties, (4) access, (5) security, (6) data integrity, and (7) enforcement.

30.   A system log should record which events?

A.   Valid logins and invalid login attempts
B.   Database errors
C.   Application errors
D.   Device driver failures

ANSWER: D. A system log records events that are logged by the operating system and its components, such as device drivers. A security log is used to track security-related information on a computer system. The security log typically contains records of login/logout activity and other security-related events specified by the system's audit policy. An application log records events that are triggered by the applications used on a computer system, such as database applications. Events that are written to the application log are determined by the developers of the software program.

31. Which of the following accurately describes an organization's ability to monitor its employees in the EU?

   A. Employee monitoring is permitted only within the physical areas owned by the organization
   B. Employee monitoring is never permitted
   C. Employee monitoring is permitted only with the express written consent of the employee
   D. Employee monitoring is permitted only when necessary for a specific purpose

ANSWER: D. In Europe, once an employer decides to monitor an employee, the Article 29 Working Party suggests that the organization follow the following seven basic principles: (1) an employer must determine whether the monitoring is absolutely necessary for the specified purpose, (2) data collected through the monitoring must respond to a "specified, explicit and legitimate" purpose and cannot be processed for a different purpose, (3) the employer must provide clear and open notice to employees about the monitoring, (4) employers may monitor only to safeguard their legitimate interests, while not violating an employee's fundamental rights, (5) personal data processed in connection with the monitoring must be adequate, relevant, and not excessive, (6) personal data must be updated and retained only for the period deemed necessary for the purpose to be achieved, and (7) the employer must implement all appropriate technical and organizational measures to ensure that any personal data is protected from alteration, unauthorized access, and misuse.

32. Which of the following accurately describes the provisions of the EU e-Privacy Directive?

   A. The Directive takes an opt-out approach to unsolicited commercial electronic communications
   B. The Directive takes an opt-in approach to unsolicited commercial electronic communications
   C. The Directive requires express written consent for marketing to minors
   D. The Directive allows inferred consent for marketing to minors

ANSWER: B. The EU e-Privacy Directive takes an opt-in approach to unsolicited commercial electronic communications (that is, users must provide their prior consent before such communications are addressed to them). The Directive does not expressly address marketing to minors.

33. What is the effect of incorporating the standard contractual clauses of a model contract approved by the EU Commission into an international agreement between a data controller located in Germany and a data processor incorporated in the United States?

A. Personal data may flow from the data processor to the data controller
B. Personal data may flow from the data controller to the data processor
C. The data controller is now a company providing an adequate level of protection
D. The data controller may now transfer personal data within the EU member states

ANSWER: B. After incorporating the standard contractual clauses of a model contract into an agreement, personal data may flow from a data controller established in any of the 27 EU member states and three EEA member countries (Norway, Liechtenstein and Iceland) to a data controller or to a data processor established in a country not ensuring an adequate level of data protection, such as the United States. The EU Commission has so far issued two sets of standard contractual clauses for transfers to data controllers established outside the EU/EEA and one set of contractual clauses to data processors established outside the EU/EEA. Answer A is incorrect because model contracts affect the ability to transfer personal data out of the EU and into countries that do not provide an adequate level of protection. Answer C is incorrect because as a data controller in Germany operating under German law the data controller is already operating in a country that provides an adequate level of protection. Answer D is incorrect because the data controller is capable of transmitting personal data within the EU by virtue of being in compliance with German law and a model contract is not needed. Again, model contracts permit the transfer of personal information from the EU into countries not providing an adequate level of protection, such as the United States.

34. Which of the following is NOT an exception to the EU Data Protection Directive's requirement that transfers of personal data may only be made to countries which ensure an adequate level of protection?

   A. The transfer is necessary for the performance of a contract between the data subject and the controller
   B. The transfer is necessary in order to protect the vital interests of the data subject
   C. The transfer is necessary or legally required on important public interest grounds
   D. The transfer is made to the data subject's next of kin or guardian

ANSWER: D. Article 26(1) of the EU Data Protection Directive states that transfers of personal data to a country which do not ensure an adequate level of protection may take place if the data subject has "given his consent unambiguously to the proposed transfer." Other exceptions include: (1) the transfer is necessary for the performance of a contract between the data subject and the controller, (2) the transfer is necessary for the conclusion or performance of a contract concluded in the interest of the data subject, (3) the transfer is necessary or legally required on important public interest grounds, and (4) the transfer is necessary in order to protect the vital interests of the data subject. Answers A, B, and C set forth valid exceptions. Transfers to the data subject's next of kin or guardian are not exempted.

35.   Which of the following is a major criticism of comprehensive privacy and data protection laws?

    A.   Cost of compliance outweighs the benefits in many industries
    B.   Incompatible with the regimes of other countries
    C.   Encourages innovation in data processing
    D.   Do not adequately protect personal information of minors

ANSWER: A. The main criticism of comprehensive privacy and data protection laws is that the cost of compliance outweighs the benefits in many industries. For example, onerous laws protecting sensitive information, such as health information, may be warranted in some cases, but the same level of protection may not be needed for less sensitive information in other industries. A second major criticism of comprehensive privacy and data protection laws is that they discourage innovation in data processing because regulatory approval is first needed before organizations may use personal information in potentially innovative ways (for example, with online social networking). These regulatory hurdles may discourage innovation.

36.   Which of the following are the main reasons why countries adopt comprehensive privacy and data protection laws?

A.   To secure international approval and combat online piracy
B.   To combat online piracy and protect personal freedoms
C.   To increase the costs of entering into a new market and remedy past injustices
D.   To remedy past injustices and encourage electronic commerce

ANSWER: D. Remedying past injustices and encourage electronic commerce are two of the main reasons that countries enact comprehensive privacy and data protection laws. Countries also enact comprehensive privacy laws to ensure consistency with other comprehensive regimes, such as the EU and its Data Protection Directive. Securing international approval, combating online piracy, protecting personal freedoms, and increasing the costs of entering into a new market are not the main reasons why countries adopt comprehensive privacy laws.

37.   Which country has NOT joined the European Economic Area ("EEA") but is part of the European Free Trade Association ("EFTA")?

A.   Switzerland
B.   Norway
C.   Liechtenstein
D.   Iceland

ANSWER: A. Switzerland rejected the EEA agreement in a national referendum on December 6, 1992. Switzerland is, however, a current member of EFTA (along with Norway, Liechtenstein, and Iceland).

38.　Which of the following may be considered personal information?

　A.　Information about an organization's competitors
　B.　Information about a company's financial well being
　C.　Information about an organization's business leads or prospects
　D.　Information about a company's physical address

ANSWER: C. Personal information is any information about an identified or identifiable individual. An organization's customers and prospects may be individuals, and therefore information about them may be classified as personal information. The other answer choices all relate to information about an organization (as opposed to an individual), and therefore are not types of personal information.

39.　Which country's privacy laws set forth specific and detailed requirements for the data protection officer ("DPO") of an organization?

　A.　Germany
　B.　Canada
　C.　New Zealand
　D.　Australia

ANSWER: A. A data protection officer ("DPO") is an individual (or group of individuals) responsible for data protection and privacy issues at an organization. Many organizations in Germany are obligated to formally appoint a data protection officer. Generally, companies that permanently employ ten or more persons in the automated processing of personal data are required to appoint a DPO. Each DPO must have intimate knowledge of Germany's data protection laws and possess other defined skills. Noncompliance may results in administrative fines for the organization. Most countries other than Germany do not have specific requirements for the DPO.

40. What was one of the primary purposes of the 2009 Madrid Resolution regarding the International Standards on the Protection of Personal Data and Privacy?

   A. To protect minors from the unauthorized collection of personal information
   B. To define a set of principles and rights guaranteeing the effective and internationally uniform protection of privacy
   C. To establish penalties for those responsible for violating the privacy rights of individuals
   D. To limit the use of automated processing of personal data

ANSWER: B. The stated purposes of the International Standards on the Protection of Personal Data and Privacy, which was adopted as part of the 2009 Madrid Resolution, are to (1) define a set of principles and rights guaranteeing the effective and internationally uniform protection of privacy with regards to the processing of personal data and (2) facilitate the international flow of personal data needed in a globalized world.

41. Which of the following is NOT a principle of the Asia-Pacific Economic Cooperation ("APEC") Privacy Framework adopted in 2004?

A. Preventing harm
B. Notice
C. Active enforcement
D. Collection limitation

ANSWER: D. The Asia-Pacific Economic Cooperation ("APEC") Privacy Framework, which is consistent with the OECD's 1980 Guidelines, has the following principles: (1) preventing harm, (2) notice, (3) collection limitation, (4) uses of personal information, (5) choice, (6) integrity of personal information, (7) security safeguards, (8) access and correction, and (9) accountability.

42. Which of the following accurately describes the use of public-key cryptography?

A. Sender uses recipient's public key to encrypt and receiver uses his public key to decrypt
B. Sender uses sender's private key to encrypt and receiver uses sender's public key to decrypt
C. Sender uses recipient's private key to encrypt and receiver uses his public key to decrypt
D. Sender uses recipient's public key to encrypt and receiver uses his private key to decrypt

ANSWER: D. Public-key cryptography (also called asymmetric-key cryptography) uses a pair of keys to encrypt and decrypt content. Each user has a pair of cryptographic keys – a public encryption key and a private decryption key. The public key is widely distributed, while the private key is known only to its owner. The keys are related mathematically, but the parameters used to generate the keys are chosen so that calculating the private key from the public key is virtually impossible.

43. What type of log should record events related to a database?

   A. Security log
   B. System log
   C. Application log
   D. Device log

ANSWER: C. An application log records events that are triggered by the applications used on a computer system, such as a database application. Events that are written to the application log are determined by the developers of the software program, not the operating system. A security log is used to track security-related information on a computer system. The security log typically contains records of login/logout activity and other security-related events specified by the system's audit policy. A system log contains events that are logged by the operating system and its components, such as device drivers.

44. Which type of security measure may be used to prevent a cookie poisoning attack?

   A. Encryption
   B. Firewall
   C. Intrusion detection system
   D. Antivirus software

ANSWER: A. Cookie poisoning is the modification of a web cookie by an attacker in hopes of gaining unauthorized information about the user for illegitimate purposes, such as identity theft. To guard against cookie poisoning, websites that use cookies should protect them (for example, through encryption) before they are sent to a user's computer.

45. The EU Commission has classified which of the following countries as providing an adequate level of privacy protection?

   A. Israel
   B. Australia
   C. Argentina
   D. Morocco

ANSWER: C. The European Commission has classified the following major countries as providing an adequate level of privacy protection: Switzerland, Canada, Andorra, Argentina, Iceland, Liechtenstein, and Israel.

46. Which country takes a co-regulatory approach to privacy?

    A.   Germany
    B.   Australia
    C.   Zimbabwe
    D.   Morocco

ANSWER: B. Canada, Australia, and New Zealand are three major countries employing a co-regulatory model of privacy protection.

47. Which of the following is NOT a requirement of the Personal Information Protection and Electronic Documents Act ("PIPEDA")?

    A.   Organizations covered by the Act must obtain an individual's consent when they collect, use or disclose the individual's personal information
    B.   The individual has a right to access personal information held by an organization and to challenge its accuracy
    C.   Personal information can only be used for the purposes for which it was collected
    D.   Organizations covered by the Act must provide an annual privacy notice to their customers

ANSWER: D. PIPEDA is a Canadian data privacy law that codifies the fair information principles. Therefore, A, B, and C are requirements of the Act. Annual privacy notices are not required as long as an organization's rules for processing personal information are clear and transparent.

48. Which of the following statements accurately describes the information quality principle?

A. Information should only be accessible to those with a need to know
B. Information should be accurate, complete, and relevant to the purposes of the processing
C. Sensitive information should be protected with greater security measures than non-sensitive information
D. Information should be destroyed when it is no longer needed

ANSWER: B. Information quality is evaluated according to three metrics: (1) accuracy, (2) completeness, and (3) relevancy. Although the other answers all convey general information security principles, only answer B is directly related to information quality.

49. Which of the following is NOT a principle of privacy by design?

A. Opt-in choice
B. Privacy as the default setting
C. Proactive not reactive
D. End to end security

ANSWER: A. The Information and Privacy Commissioner of Ontario, Canada developed the privacy by design framework in the 1990s. It includes the following seven principles: (1) Proactive not Reactive; Preventative not Remedial; (2) Privacy as the Default Setting; (3) Privacy Embedded into

Design, (4) Full Functionality — Positive-Sum, not Zero-Sum; (5) End-to-End Security — Full Lifecycle Protection; (6)Visibility and Transparency — Keep it Open; and (7) Respect for User Privacy — Keep it User-Centric. Opt-in choice is not a principle of privacy by design.

50. Which of the following is NOT a main reason for organizations to protect personal information?

A. Prevention of data breaches
B. Compliance with regulations
C. Increased cost
D. Avoidance of lawsuits

ANSWER: C. Increased cost is not a reason for organizations to protect personal information. Prevention of data breaches, compliance with laws and regulations, and avoidance of lawsuits and regulatory actions are the main drivers for protecting personal information. Additional reasons for protecting personal information include (1) meeting customer expectations and (2) building a positive reputation.

51. Article 8 of the European Convention on Human Rights ("ECHR") provides protection for what privacy right?

A. Electronic communications
B. DNA profile
C. IP address
D. Private and family life

ANSWER: D. Article 8 of the ECHR provides a right of respect for a person's "private and family life," subject to certain restrictions.

52. Falsifying or "spoofing" a network address so that information is sent to an attacker as opposed to its intended recipient is an example of what type of attack?

    A.   Robust attack
    B.   Redundant attack
    C.   Network layer attack
    D.   Application layer attack

ANSWER: C. Network layer attacks are those that exploit the networking protocol. Spoofing and denial of service ("DoS") attacks are two types of network layer attacks. Application layer attacks exploit applications running on network servers, such as email and database applications. Application layer attacks are the most common type of attacks because any given network may have dozens of network applications that may be exploited.

53. Which security mechanism is used for preventing unauthorized access to internal networks?

    A.   Firewall
    B.   Encryption
    C.   Intrusion detection system
    D.   Antivirus software

ANSWER: A. Firewalls are software or hardware solutions that prevent certain types of network traffic from entering an internal network in accordance with the firewall's policy. The other types of security mechanisms provided do not prevent unauthorized access to internal networks.

54. Which of following organizations does NOT provide industry standard best practices for information security?

   A. International Organization for Standardization ("ISO")
   B. National Institute of Standards in Technology ("NIST")
   C. IT Governance Institute
   D. Association of Computer Engineers and Technician ("ACET")

ANSWER: D. The ISO, NIST, and IT Governance Institute are all organizations that provide standards for information security best practices.

55. What is the most common form of monitoring employed in an information security system?

   A. Intrusion detection systems
   B. System logs
   C. Key loggers
   D. Video monitoring

ANSWER: B. System logs that record security related events, such as valid and invalid logins, are the most common form of monitoring in an information security system.

56. What is the initial step when creating an effective information security system for an existing organization?

   A.   Define the security policy
   B.   Select controls for managing risk
   C.   Identify, analyze, and evaluate risk
   D.   Conduct an information assessment

ANSWER: D. An information assessment is the first step when creating an effective information security system at an organization. Before a privacy practitioner can develop an information security system, he must assess what information is currently being collected at the organization and what information technology systems are being used to process the information. Only after the practitioner has a solid understanding of the information and systems in place can he develop an effective information security system.

57. What step should be performed first after defining the security policy when creating an information security program?

   A.   Monitor and periodically review the security program
   B.   Select controls for managing risk
   C.   Identify, analyze, and evaluate risk
   D.   Establish the scope of the information security system

ANSWER: C. The basic procedure for creating an information security program is (1) establish the scope of the information security system, (2) define the security policy, (3) establish a protocol for risk assessment, (4) identify, analyze, and evaluate risk, (5) select controls for managing the identified risk, (6) obtain management approval of any residual risk, and (7) monitor and periodically review the security program.

58. Which of the following is NOT a main source of information security requirements?

A. Customer complaints and recommendations
B. Threats and vulnerabilities of an organization
C. Legal, regulatory, and contractual obligations
D. An organization's information security and privacy policies

ANSWER: A. Customer complaints and recommendations are not a main source of security requirements. Generally, an organization should have reasonable security protecting personal information based on the C-I-A triad. To provide reasonable security, threats and vulnerabilities of an organization must be analyzed to determine the level of risk. Laws, regulations, and contracts that an organization has entered into generally contain security requirements for an organization. An organization's information security and privacy policies also generally include security requirements for different classes of information held or collected by the organization.

59. What is the relationship between information security and information privacy?

   A. Information security is concerned only with the unauthorized access of personal information, whereas information privacy addresses the use and confidentiality of personal information
   B. Information security is a necessary component of information privacy
   C. Information privacy is a subset of information security
   D. Information security is concerned with the unauthorized access, use, and confidentiality of personal information, whereas information privacy addresses only the use of personal information

ANSWER: B. Both information security and information privacy deal with the access, use, and confidentiality of information. Information security is one necessary component of information privacy. Information privacy also addresses the data subject's rights with respect to the personal information (for example, the right to correct and control processing of his personal information).

60. In which cloud computer service model do users rent computing resources, such as storage, network capacity, and other resources?

   A. Software as a service (SaaS)
   B. Platform as a service (PaaS)
   C. Infrastructure as a service (IaaS)
   D. Hardware as a service (HaaS)

ANSWER: C. IaaS is the most basic cloud service model. In IaaS, users rent computing resources, such as storage, network capacity, and processing power from cloud providers. The cloud provider owns the equipment and is responsible for housing, running, and maintaining it. Under PaaS, cloud providers deliver a computing platform, typically including an operating system, database, and web server. Web developers build and publish web applications using the platform. Finally, with SaaS, applications are hosted by the cloud vendor in the cloud. Customers typically access the applications through a web browser over the Internet. SaaS is often referred to as "on-demand software."

61. Which organization is developing standards for a Do Not Track approach to online targeted advertising?

   A. International Organization for Standardization ("ISO")
   B. Federal Trade Commission ("FTC")
   C. World Wide Web Consortium ("W3C")
   D. National Institute of Standards and Technology ("NIST")

ANSWER: C. The Tracking Protection Working Group of the W3C is developing standards for online targeted advertising, including a Do Not Track specification.

62.	The EU e-Privacy Directive requires what type of consent before a cookie may be placed on a user's computer?

A.	Written consent
B.	Affirmative consent
C.	Opt-out consent
D.	Parental consent

ANSWER: B. The EU e-Privacy Directive requires affirmative, opt-in consent for cookies. Specifically, the Directive requires that "the subscriber or user concerned has given his or her consent, having been provided with clear and comprehensive information."

63.	The National Advertising Initiative ("NAI") manages a self-regulatory pledge related to which of the following?

A.	Direct mail marketing
B.	Commercial email advertising
C.	Sponsored search results
D.	Online targeted advertising

ANSWER: D. The NAI's Code of Conduct is a set of self-regulatory principles that require NAI member companies to provide notice and choice with respect to Interest-based advertising, and specifically online targeted advertising. Advertising networks which satisfy the NAI principles must provide consumers a choice about whether information collected about them is tracked and used to provide targeted advertising.

64. The Do Not Call Registry applies to what type of marketing?

A. Email marketing
B. Telemarketing
C. Unsolicited commercial messages
D. Educational marketing

ANSWER: B. Pursuant to its authority under the Telephone Consumer Protection Act ("TCPA"), the Federal Communication Commission ("FCC") established, together with the Federal Trade Commission ("FTC"), a national Do Not Call Registry in 2003. The registry is nationwide in scope, applies to all telemarketers (with the exception of certain non-profit organizations), and covers both interstate and intrastate telemarketing calls. Commercial telemarketers are not allowed to call you if your number is on the registry, subject to certain exceptions.

65. Which of the following statements concerning PIPEDA is false?

A. PIPEDA applies only to private organizations
B. Under PIPEDA, an organization may disclose personal information without the consent of the data subject for debt collection purposes
C. The Commissioner may audit any organization collecting personal information on Canadian citizens
D. An organization may use personal information without consent of the data subject in emergency situations

ANSWER: A. PIPEDA applies to every organization across Canada that collects, uses, or discloses personal information in the course of commercial activities. Therefore, PIPEDA regulates both public and private organizations.

66. Data protection laws in Latin America are largely based on what principle?

    A. Ombudsmen
    B. Sensitive categories of data
    C. Habeas data
    D. Data protection authorities

ANSWER: C. Habeas data is a writ and constitutional remedy available in most Latin American countries. The literal translation from Latin of habeas data is "you have the data." The remedy varies from country to country, but in general, it is designed to protect, by means of an individual complaint presented to a constitutional court, the image, privacy, honor, and freedom of information of a person.

67. Which of the following is false regarding European privacy laws?

  A. European law is based on the tenant that privacy is a fundamental right
  B. The EU Data Protection Directive authorizes transfer of personal data to countries outside the EU if the country provides an adequate level of protection
  C. The EU Data Protection Directive applies to all sectors of industry and all types of personal information
  D. The EU Data Protection Directive substantially increased Switzerland's controls over financial data

ANSWER: D. The EU Data Protection Directive applies to countries of the European Economic Area ("EEA"), which includes all EU countries, and in addition, the non-EU countries Iceland, Liechtenstein, and Norway. Switzerland rejected the EEA agreement and therefore is not bound by the EU Data Protection Directive. Switzerland has, however, passed a comprehensive data privacy that has been deemed adequate by the European Commission.

68. Which state was the first to enact rules governing the use and disclosure of consumer energy information from smart grids in the United States?

  A. California
  B. Florida
  C. Connecticut
  D. Massachusetts

ANSWER: A. The smart grid is an advanced metering system made up of smart meters capable of recording detailed and real-time data on consumer electricity usage that is then sent to a central hub for processing. In 2011, the California Public Utilities Commission ("CPUC") established privacy rules for California's Smart Grid that covered the collection of customer usage data from the electricity grid.

69. In which country is a person's salary considered a public record?

A. Canada
B. Sweden
C. China
D. Argentina

ANSWER: B. In Sweden, tax returns are considered public records. Included within the tax return is a person's salary. Finland and Norway also treat tax returns as public records.

70. Which data element has recently become important because of the increasing use of smart phones?

A. Voice recordings
B. Telephone records
C. IP address
D. Location

ANSWER: D. Location is a data element that is becoming increasingly important from a privacy perspective. Smart phones and other telecommunications devices can determine your location in real-time to uniquely identify a person.

71. What is the original purpose of bank secrecy laws?

A. To enable banks to better share information
B. To protect customer's financial information
C. To permit access of financial data by government authority for national security purposes
D. To ensure creditors have appropriate access to a debtor's financial information

ANSWER: B. Bank secrecy is a legal principle in some jurisdictions under which banks are not allowed to provide to authorities personal and account information about their customers unless certain conditions apply (for example, a criminal complaint has been filed). Bank secrecy laws are routinely criticized because they may enable money laundering.

72. Which of the following is correct regarding the Gramm-Leach-Bliley Act of 1999 ("GLBA")?

   A. The Act is based on the permissible purpose approach to privacy
   B. The Act covers all financial information, including publicly available information
   C. The Act requires opt-in consent when sharing financial information with unaffiliated third parties
   D. The Act established a complicated set of privacy and security requirements for all financial institutions

ANSWER: D. The GLBA is based on the fair information practices approach to privacy and not the permissible use approach. The GLBA also does not cover publicly available financial information, and the sharing of financial data with unaffiliated third parties is permitted with opt-out consent. Therefore, answer D is the best choice.

73. This country takes a co-regulatory approach to privacy protection similar to that of Australia?

   A. Israel
   B. New Zealand
   C. Zimbabwe
   D. Morocco

ANSWER: B. Canada, Australia, and New Zealand are three countries employing a co-regulatory model of privacy protection.

74. After the Article 29 Working Party favorably evaluated this county's privacy law in 2010, the European Commission formally approved this country as providing an adequate level of protection in 2012?

A. Uruguay
B. Mexico
C. Hong Kong
D. Japan

ANSWER: A. Uruguay was deemed adequate in 2012. Before Uruguay, the Working Party favorably evaluated Israel in 2009, and the European Commission formally approved Israel as providing adequate protection in 2011.

75. Japan's Act on the Protection of Personal Information Act defines "principal" as which entity?

A. Data processor
B. Data controller
C. Data subject
D. Data importer

ANSWER: C. In accordance with Japan's Protection of Personal Information Act, the term "principal" or "person" is the specific individual identified by the personal information (that is, the data subject).

76. Which Middle East country requires that databases of more than 10,000 persons be registered with the government?

A. Iran
B. Israel
C. Egypt
D. Iraq

ANSWER: B. Israel's Protection of Privacy law requires registration of any database that includes information about more than 10,000 persons. More specifically, it requires registration of a database if (1) the database includes information about more than 10,000 persons; (2) the database includes sensitive information; (3) the database includes information about persons and the information was not provided to the database by them, on their behalf or with their consent; (4) the database belongs to a public body; or (5) the database is used for direct mail. In 2011, the EU Commission decided that Israel is a country providing an adequate level of protection.

77. Which of the following is NOT exempt from disclosure under the Freedom of Information Act ("FOIA")?

A. Records containing trade secrets
B. Records containing the location of oil wells
C. Records describing the data handling practices of financial institutions
D. Records pertaining to federal regulatory agencies, federal employees, and federal agents

ANSWER: D. FOIA has the following nine exemptions: (1) those documents properly classified as secret in the interest of national defense or foreign policy; (2) related solely to internal personnel rules and practices; (3) specifically exempted by other statutes; (4) a trade secret or privileged or confidential commercial or financial information obtained from a person; (5) a privileged inter-agency or intra-agency memorandum or letter; (6) a personnel, medical, or similar file the release of which would constitute a clearly unwarranted invasion of personal privacy; (7) compiled for law enforcement purposes; (8) contained in or related to examination, operating, or condition reports about financial institutions; and (9) those documents containing exempt information about gas or oil wells. Answers A, B, and C fall in exemptions (4), (9), and (8), respectively. Answer D is not a recognized exemption and therefore is the correct answer.

78. The Children's Online Privacy Protection Act ("COPPA") prevents website operators from performing what activity?

A. Creating a website with content designed for children under 13 years of age
B. Collecting personal information from children under 13 years of age
C. Displaying a picture of a child after obtaining verifiable parental consent
D. Operating a website that is geared towards children in the United States with storage servers located outside the United States

ANSWER: B. Generally, COPPA applies to the online collection of personal information from children under

13 years of age. COPPA details what a website operator must include in a privacy policy, when and how to seek verifiable consent from a parent or guardian, and what responsibilities an operator has to protect children's privacy and safety online, including restrictions on the marketing to those under 13 years of age.

79. Which of the following is the most appropriate mechanism for enabling a multinational European corporation to transfer data concerning EU residents from Europe to one of its offices in the United States?

   A.   Binding corporate rules
   B.   Contractual assurances
   C.   U.S. Safe Harbor program
   D.   Implicit consent

ANSWER: A. Binding corporate rules ("BCR") are internal rules adopted by a multinational group of related companies which define its global policy with regard to the international transfers of personal data within the same corporate group to entities located in countries which do not provide an adequate level of protection. Because the EU Commission has not deemed the U.S. as providing an adequate level of protection, a multinational corporation in Europe may adopt binding corporate rules with its offices in the U.S. to comply with the EU Data Protection Directive.

80.   What is one of the primary purposes of the
      FCRA?

   A.   Give employers the right to correct credit
        reports for their employees
   B.   Encourage the dissemination of consumer
        data to foreign companies with a need to
        know the data
   C.   Limit the use of consumer reports to
        permissible purposes
   D.   Allow data reporters to place a debt on a
        consumer's credit report if they have a
        reasonable suspicion of the debt

ANSWER: C. Under the FCRA, a consumer report may
only be acquired for a "permissible purpose." Section
604 of the FCRA sets forth the circumstances that are
considered permissible, including with the written
instructions of the consumer to whom the credit report
relates.

81.   When transferring personal data from Europe to
      the United States, which type of consent in
      needed from the data subjects?

   A.   Implied consent
   B.   Unambiguous consent
   C.   General consent
   D.   Advance consent

ANSWER: B. Article 26(1) of the EU Data Protection
Directive states that transfers of personal data to a
third countries which do not ensure an adequate level
of protection may take place if the data subject has
"given his consent unambiguously to the proposed
transfer." Other exceptions include: (1) the transfer is

necessary for the performance of a contract between the data subject and the controller, (2) the transfer is necessary for the conclusion or performance of a contract concluded in the interest of the data subject, (3) the transfer is necessary or legally required on important public interest grounds, and (4) the transfer is necessary in order to protect the vital interests of the data subject.

82. In accordance with the EU Data Protection Directive, unambiguous consent is achieved through what action?

   A. An advanced waiver of right
   B. An express verbal indication
   C. Any freely given specific and informed indication
   D. None of the above

ANSWER: C. In accordance with the EU Data Protection Directive, the data subject's unambiguous consent means "any freely given specific and informed indication of his wishes by which the data subject signifies his agreement to personal data relating to him being processed."

83. Which regulatory agency does NOT enforce or certify compliance with the U.S. Safe Harbor program?

   A. FTC
   B. Department of Transportation
   C. FCC
   D. Department of Commerce

ANSWER: C. The European Union ("EU") Data Protection Directive prohibits the transfer of personal data to non-European Union countries that do not meet the European Union (EU) "adequacy" standard for privacy protection. While the United States and the EU share the goal of enhancing privacy protection for their citizens, the United States takes a different approach to privacy than that of the EU. The U.S. Department of Commerce in consultation with the European Commission developed the Safe Harbor framework to bridge these differences in approach and provide a streamlined means for U.S. organizations to comply with the Directive. Only U.S. organizations subject to the jurisdiction of the Federal Trade Commission ("FTC") or U.S. air carriers and ticket agents subject to the jurisdiction of the Department of Transportation ("DoT") may participate in the Safe Harbor program. The FTC and DoT enforce the program while the Department of Commerce receives annually certifications of compliance from those organizations participating in the program.

84. Which of the following is not considered an example of the self-regulatory model of data protection?

    A. Payment Card Industry Data Security Standard ("PCI DSS")
    B. Online Privacy Alliance
    C. TRUSTe
    D. ISO 27001

ANSWER: D. ISO 27001 specifies a management system that is intended to bring information security under explicit management control. ISO 27001 requires that management (1) systematically examine the organization's information security risks, (2) design and implement a coherent and comprehensive suite of information security controls to address those risks, and (3) adopt an overarching management process to ensure that the selected information security controls continue to meet the organization's information security needs on an ongoing basis. ISO 27001 (unlike PCI DSS, the Online Privacy Alliance, and TRUSTe), is not an example of the self-regulatory model of data protection.

85. When should a privacy impact assessment occur?

    A.   After implementation of a new project
    B.   When a system holding personal information is decommissioned
    C.   Before the onset of a new project and periodically thereafter
    D.   Each fiscal year

ANSWER: C. A privacy impact assessment is an analysis of how information is processed to ensure the processing conforms to all applicable legal, regulatory, and policy requirements. An assessment should be completed before implementation of a privacy project and should be ongoing through its deployment.

86. What is an important part of a privacy impact assessment?

    A.   Identifying the types of information that are to be collected
    B.   Controlling access to the results of the assessment
    C.   Conducting the assessment immediately after a new project is implemented
    D.   Ensuring that technical safeguards are protecting all personal information

ANSWER: A. During a privacy impact assessment, the data being collected and its attributes must be closely analyzed. Specifically, what type of data is being collected, for what purpose, for how long, with whom is the data being shared, and the choices available to the data subject regarding processing should be considered and analyzed.

87. Which of the following management operations are consistent with lifecycle principles?

    A.   Pseudonymize and aggregation; monitoring and enforcement
    B.   Anonymization and aggregation; archival and retrieval
    C.   Transfer and encryption; monitoring and enforcement
    D.   Management and administration; monitoring and enforcement

ANSWER: D. The information lifecycle consists of (1) collection, (2) use, (3) disclosure, and (4) retention or destruction. Associated with the information lifecycle are the management processes needed to effectively implement an organization's information privacy policies and procedures. Specifically, an organization should manage and administer any defined privacy policy, while also monitoring and enforcing compliance with the policy. Without these management related activities, information cannot be adequately protected throughout its lifecycle.

88. The United States takes what approach to privacy protection?

   A.   Comprehensive
   B.   Sectoral
   C.   Co-regulatory
   D.   Self-regulatory

ANSWER: B. The United States and Japan take a sectoral approach to privacy protection in which sector specific laws are enacted as opposed to a general, more comprehensive data protection law. The EU is a notable jurisdiction with a comprehensive privacy law. Canada, Australia, and New Zealand are three major countries employing a co-regulatory model of privacy protection.

89. Which of the following is a type of administrative safeguard for personal information?

   A.   Incident response procedures
   B.   Password authentication
   C.   Locks for portable computing devices
   D.   Firewalls

ANSWER: A. Administrative safeguards are administrative actions, policies, and procedures that protect personal information. An incident response plan or procedure is a type of administrative safeguard. Password authentication and firewalls are types of physical safeguards, while locks are physical safeguards.

90. Which of the following is NOT a form of communication that can be used as a privacy notice?

A. Web pages
B. Icons
C. Signs
D. Product listings with prices

ANSWER: D. Privacy notices may come in many different forms. In fact, any form of communication that reasonably conveys privacy-related information may be used to communicate a privacy notice. Web pages, icons, and signs are all forms of commonly used privacy notices. An organization's product listings would not constitute a privacy notice.

91. The Interactive Advertising Bureau ("IAB") uses a privacy policy in the form of what for behavior tracking?

A. Contract
B. Icon
C. Sign
D. Brochure

ANSWER: B. The IAB has developed a comprehensive self-regulatory program for online behavioral advertising. The program promotes the use of an icon and accompanying language to be displayed in or near online advertisements or on web pages where data is collected and used for behavioral advertising.

92. What are the two primary purposes of a privacy notice?

A. Trust and corporate accountability
B. Consumer education and corporate accountability
C. Trust and compliance
D. Compliance and consumer education

ANSWER: B. The primary purpose of a privacy notice is to educate the consumer about an organization's privacy practices and the options that the consumer has with respect to processing of the consumer's personal information. The secondary purpose is to hold organizations accountable for following the terms and conditions specified in their privacy notice. If an organization fails to comply with its privacy notice, it may be held liable by the FTC for a deceptive trade practice. When companies state that they will safeguard personal information, the FTC can and does take law enforcement action to make sure that companies live up to these promises.

93. Which of the following is NOT considered personal information about an employee held by the human resources department of an employer?

A.   Sick leave requests
B.   Salary
C.   Title
D.   Performance evaluations

ANSWER: C. Personal information is any information about an identified or identifiable individual. Sick leave requests, salary, and performance evaluations are typically unique to a particular person and therefore constitute personal information. An employee's job title, on the other hand, is not typically unique. Accordingly, a title is not generally considered personal data. In other words, "title" is the data element least likely to uniquely identify an individual and therefore is the correct answer.

94. Which of the following is NOT considered personal information about a customer held by a retailer?

A.   Order history
B.   Voice recordings from correspondence with the customer
C.   Purchase history
D.   Top selling products

ANSWER: D. Personal information is any information about an identified or identifiable individual. A company's top selling products is generally derived from aggregated data that is not considered personal data. All other answers described information that would typically uniquely identify an individual and therefore is personal information.

95. Which of the following is an example of personal information from a public record in the United States?

   A.   Heath plan number from an insurance card
   B.   Name and address of an owner of a piece of real estate from a real estate deed
   C.   Driver's license number from a government issued citation
   D.   Genetic information from a private genome project

ANSWER: B. Public records are information collected and maintained by the government and that are available to the public. Public records include real estate deeds, birth and marriage certificates, tax liens, and other data recorded by the government and made available for public inspection.

96. Which of the following is a privacy implication of an IPv6 internet address?

   A.   IPv6 allows for fewer IP address than its predecessor IPv4
   B.   IPv6 and IPv4 are interoperable
   C.   IPv6 is less secure than an IPv4 address
   D.   IPv6 use a new addressing scheme that may make it easier to associate an address with a specific individual

ANSWER: D. IPv6 uses 128-bit addresses, resulting in approximately 3.4×10^{38} unique addresses, or more than 7.9×10^{28} times as many addresses as IPv4, which uses only 32-bit addresses. In IPv4, the effort to conserve address space with network address translation ("NAT") helped obfuscate network address spaces, hosts, and topologies, thereby increasing privacy protection. In IPv6, however, when using address auto-configuration, the interface identifier (or MAC address) of an interface port is used to make its public IP address unique, potentially exposing the type of hardware used and providing a unique handle for a user's online activity. Therefore, IPv6's new addressing scheme may make it easier to associate an address with a specific individual, thereby creating a privacy concern.

97. The EU Data Protection Directive uses what term to refer to sensitive personal information?

A. Special categories of data
B. Inherently protected data
C. Classified data types
D. Intrinsic data

ANSWER: A. The EU Data Protection Directive uses the term "special categories of data" to describe sensitive personal information. In accordance with the Directive, special categories of data include personal data revealing racial or ethnic origin, political opinions, religious or philosophical beliefs, trade-union membership, and the processing of data concerning health or sex life.

98.   In the EU, which of the following types of information is considered a special category of data?

A.   Country identification number
B.   Gender
C.   Political opinions
D.   Driver's license number

ANSWER: C. The EU Data Protection Directive uses the term "special categories of data" to describe sensitive personal information. In accordance with the Directive, special categories of data include personal data revealing racial or ethnic origin, political opinions, religious or philosophical beliefs, trade-union membership, and the processing of data concerning health or sex life.

99.   Which of the following types of information is always considered non-personal data?

A.   Email addresses
B.   Gender
C.   Salary
D.   Aggregated data

ANSWER: D. Personal data is any data that describes an identified or identifiable individual. "Anonymized," "de-identified," and "aggregated" data are types of non-personal data because the data cannot be traced back to an identified or identifiable individual.

100. When may information about an organization be considered personal information?

A. When the organization is a sole proprietorship
B. When the organization is multi-national
C. When the organization files taxes
D. When the organization is controlled by a single Board of Director

ANSWER: A. Generally, personal information is any information describing an identified or identifiable individual (in contrast to a corporation). However, when a company is a sole proprietorship, information describing the sole proprietorship may be traceable to a specific and identifiable individual. In such cases, information about a sole proprietorship may constitute personal information.

101. Which of the following may be considered personal information?

A. Financial data of an organization
B. Intellectual property of an organization
C. Operational data of an organization
D. Human resources data of an organization

ANSWER: D. Financial data, intellectual property, and operational data are all important types of information related to an organization. However, personal information is data describing an identified or identifiable individual (in contrast to a corporation). Human resources data, on the other hand, does describe employees of an organization and therefore may constitute personal information if describing an identified or identifiable individual.

102. Which jurisdiction considers IP addresses as personal information?

A. Japan
B. Canada
C. EU
D. Australia

ANSWER: C. In the European Union, IP addresses are generally considered personal information. In fact, the Article 29 Working Party has repeatedly advised that IP addresses should be regarded as personal data, especially in those cases where the processing of IP addresses is carried out with the purpose of identifying the users of the computer.

103. Which country does not consider business contact information as personal information?

A. Argentina
B. United States
C. Australia
D. Canada

ANSWER: D. In accordance with Canada's Personal Information Protection and Electronic Documents Act ("PIPEDA"), personal information means any information about an identifiable individual, but does not include the name or business contact information (e.g., business address) of an employee of an organization.

104. Which type of personal information is universally considered sensitive personal information?

A. Human resources data
B. Health records
C. Name and address
D. Gender

ANSWER: B. In virtually all jurisdictions, health related data constitutes sensitive person information because it relates to the inner workings of a person's body and mind, which is inherently private and sensitive.

105. Which characteristic of cloud computing provides computer services, such as email, applications, network or server service, without requiring human interaction with a service provider?

A. Broad network access
B. On-demand self-service
C. Resource pooling
D. Rapid elasticity

ANSWER: B. On-demand self-service refers to the ability to access computing resources in the cloud without having to first interact with the cloud provider. Broad network access refers to the ability to connect to the cloud through a network using standard mechanisms employed on a wide range of devices. Resource pooling refers to aggregation of computing resources for use by many cloud consumers. Rapid elasticity refers to a provider's ability to automatically provision cloud resources. Finally, measured service refers to provider's ability to measure, control, and report computing resource usage so as to provide transparency for both the provider and consumer of the cloud. On-demand self-service, broad network access, resource pooling, rapid elasticity, and measured service are all characteristics of cloud computing.

106. In which service model of cloud computing do users rent storage in a virtual data center along with other resources, such as computing and network capability?

    A.   Infrastructure as a service ("IaaS")
    B.   Platform as a service ("PaaS")
    C.   Software as a service ("SaaS")
    D.   Network as a service ("NaaS")

ANSWER: A. IaaS is the most basic cloud service model. In IaaS, users rent computing resources, such as storage, network capacity, and processing power, from cloud providers. The cloud provider owns the equipment and is responsible for housing, running, and maintaining it. Under PaaS, cloud providers deliver a computing platform, typically including an operating system, database, and web server. Web developers build and publish web applications using the computing platform. Finally, with SaaS, applications are hosted by the cloud vendor in the cloud. Customers typically access the applications through a web browser over the Internet. SaaS is often referred to as "on-demand software."

107. What practice have major search engines recently employed to address privacy concerns over search data retained by the search engines?

A. Search engines are no longer storing search history data for any of their users
B. Search engines are deleting search data after one year from the search
C. Search engines are deleting search data after notification from the government
D. Search engines are anonymizing search data after a predetermined period of time

ANSWER: D. A user's browsing history is an important asset to a company running a search engine. Therefore, search companies would not readily agree to permanently deleting this data. Instead, they have taken the middle ground by anonymizing search data (including page views, page clicks, advertisement views, and advertisement clicks) after a predetermined period of time (ranging from 90 days to 24 months).

108. Which type of cookie is used to remember a user's login credentials between visits to a particular website?

A. First-party cookie
B. Persistent cookie
C. Third-party cookie
D. Session cookie

ANSWER: B. Persistent cookies, unlike session cookies, remain stored on the user's computer for a predetermined period of time and persistent beyond a user's session. Therefore, persistent cookies enable various website features, including the "remember me" functionality prevalent on most websites that automatically logs a user back into a website.

109. The EU Cookie Directive established what new principle?

A. Website operators are required to provide website users the opportunity to opt out from the use of cookies
B. Website operators are required to provide website users written notice that a cookie is placed on the user's device upon leaving the website
C. Website operators are required to obtain the user's consent before placing a cookie on the user's device
D. Cookies are classified as sensitive personal information

ANSWER: C. The EU Cookie Directive requires affirmative consent before cookies may be placed on the user's computer. Consent is defined as "any freely given specific and informed indication of his wishes by which the data subject signifies his agreement to personal data relating to him being processed."

110. The Digital Advertising Alliance has recently developed an icon program for what purpose?

  A. To develop effective self-regulatory principles for online behavioral advertising
  B. To prevent websites from using first-party cookies
  C. To create a set of procedures for increasing an advertising campaign's return on investment
  D. To combat unsolicited electronic mail

ANSWER: A. The Digital Advertising Alliance ("DAA") Self-Regulatory Program for Online Behavioral Advertising was launched in 2010. The DAA includes a consortium of the nation's largest media and marketing associations, including the American Association of Advertising Agencies (4A's), the Association of National Advertisers (ANA), the American Advertising Federation (AAF), the Direct Marketing Association (DMA), the Interactive Advertising Bureau (IAB), and the Network Advertising Initiative (NAI). These associations and their thousands of members are committed to developing effective self-regulatory solutions to consumer choice in online behavioral advertising. Based on the seven self-regulatory principles for online behavioral advertising proposed by the Federal Trade Commission, the DAA program is designed to give consumers enhanced control over the collection and use of data regarding their Internet viewing for online behavioral advertising purposes.

111. TRUSTe, WebTrust, and BBBOnline are organizations that offer what?

    A.   Online security initiatives
    B.   Third-party authentication services
    C.   Web-based cloud computing platforms
    D.   Industry self-regulatory seal programs

ANSWER: D. TRUSTe, WebTrust, and BBBOnline all offer self-regulatory seal programs dealing with online privacy.

112. Which web form input technique should be used in accordance with information security best practices?

    A.   Scrolling text box
    B.   One-line text box
    C.   Check box for acknowledgement of a privacy policy
    D.   Radio button for acknowledgement of a privacy policy

ANSWER: C. Information security best practices dictate that a user's acknowledgement of an organization's privacy policy be indicated through the use of a check box. Check boxes allow for both opt-in and opt-out choice, which is routinely provided for in a privacy policy. Text boxes, on the other hand, are inherently less secure than check boxes and radio buttons because the user's input is not restricted. This lack of control over the user's input creates a potential security issue when using text boxes. Radio buttons are not recommended for the acknowledgement of a privacy policy because once a radio button is selected, it generally cannot be unselected by the user.

113. Which of the following is a common criticism of privacy notices?

    A.   Layered privacy notices are confusing and overly complex
    B.   Privacy notices are often written in legalese and difficult to understand
    C.   Privacy policies are not required for most websites that collect personal information
    D.   The short notice in a layered privacy notice does not provide a complete disclosure of a company's privacy policies

ANSWER: B. The goals of a privacy notice are to create transparency in an organization's data collection practices and to help users make informed decisions. Unfortunately, most users do not read privacy notices because they are drafted in a verbose and legally formalistic manner that is difficult to understand. Layered privacy notices address this concern by presenting the user with a short notice that is simple and concise. The short notice summarizes the organization's information handling practices and the choices available to users. The full privacy notice is typically accessible by a hyperlink from the short notice in case the user wants more information about the organization's privacy practices.

114. What is NOT a risk associated with spyware?

A. Spyware may enable access to resources that a user would otherwise not be able to access

B. Spyware may collect sensitive personal information, such as bank account numbers and passwords

C. Spyware may slow down a computer system and prevent normal operation of the system

D. Spyware may track a user's online activity and send it to remote parties

ANSWER: A. Spyware is software that gathers information about a person or organization without their knowledge and that may send such information to another entity without the person's consent. Spyware may also assert control over a computer without the owner's knowledge. Spyware is generally classified into four types: (1) system monitors, (2) Trojans, (3) adware, and (4) tracking cookies. Spyware presents many risks to the security of an organization's informational assets and systems. Spyware does not have the ability to grant a user access to a resource that the user is not authorized to access. Software that provides a user with access to a resource that the user is not authorized to access would generally be called an "exploit" and not spyware.

115. Which of the following is a standard protocol for the secure transmission of personal information over the Internet?

A. P3P
B. TCP
C. SSL
D. IP addresses

ANSWER: C. Transport layer security ("TLS") and its predecessor, secure sockets layer ("SSL"), are cryptographic protocols that provide secure communications over the Internet. Several versions of TLS and SSL are in widespread use in Internet applications, such as web browsing, email, Internet faxing, instant messaging, and voice-over-IP ("VoIP").

116. Which of the following is an example of social engineering?

A. The use of key loggers to record usernames and passwords
B. Injecting malicious code into a third-party website
C. Brute force password attacks
D. The use of non-technical means to gain access to restricted information

ANSWER: D. Social engineering, in the context of information security, refers to the psychological (that is, not-technical) manipulation of people with the goal of having those people perform actions or divulge confidential information.

117. Which of the following is NOT a requirement for management of an organization under ISO 27001?

A.   Systematically examine the organization's information security risks
B.   Design and implement a coherent and comprehensive suite of information security controls to address identified risks
C.   Adopt an overarching management process to ensure that information security controls continue to meet the organization's information security needs on an ongoing basis
D.   Communicate information security policies and best practices to all employees of an organization

ANSWER: D. ISO 27001 specifies a management system that is intended to bring information security under explicit management control. ISO 27001 requires that management (1) systematically examine the organization's information security risks, (2) design and implement a coherent and comprehensive suite of information security controls to address identified risks, and (3) adopt an overarching management process to ensure that the information security controls continue to meet the organization's information security needs on an ongoing basis. While it is a good practice to communicate information security policies to all employees, it is not a practice specified by ISO 27001.

118. What two technologies may be used to describe, create, and transport content online?

    A.   HTML and TCP
    B.   HTML and XML
    C.   HTML and SSL
    D.   HTML and URL

ANSWER: B. Hypertext Markup Language ("HTML") and eXtensible Markup Language ("XML") are two technologies used to describe, create, and transport online content. XML is a markup language designed to transport and store data, while HTML is a markup language designed to render and display data.

119. Which of the following is NOT a best practice for information security audits?

    A.   Audits must comply with both the information security policy and privacy policy
    B.   An organization must complete an audit of its storage and processing procedures on a regular basis
    C.   The audit must be conducted by an independent third-party
    D.   Results of the audit must be analyzed and plans formulated to remediate any deficiencies

ANSWER: C. Although information security audits may be conducted by third parties, it is not a requirement or best practice. Audits may be performed using in-house personnel. All other statements are best practices for information security audits. Specifically, audits must be in compliance with the organization's policies, as well as all applicable laws and regulations. Audits must also be completed at regular intervals to ensure deficiencies are identified in a timely manner. Finally, results of audits must be analyzed and deficiencies remediated.

120. What is part of the second step of information security incident management and the step immediately after discovery of a security breach?

   A.   Containment
   B.   Prevention
   C.   Eradication
   D.   Notification

ANSWER: A. When an information security incident occurs, an organization must know how to appropriately respond. The basic incident management and response process includes (1) incident discovery, (2) containment and analysis, (3) notification, and (4) eradication and prevention.

121. A security log should record which events?

   A.   Valid logins and invalid login attempts
   B.   Database errors
   C.   Application errors
   D.   Device driver failures

ANSWER: A. A security log is used to track security-related information on a computer system. The log typically contains records of login/logout activity and other security-related events specified by the system's audit policy. Other types of logs include application logs and system logs. A system log contains events that are logged by the operating system and its components. An application log records events that are triggered by the applications used on a computer system. Events that are written to the application log are determined by the developers of the software program, not the operating system.

122. Which of the following accurately describes the use of digital signatures to secure an email

   A. Sender uses recipient's public key and receiver uses his public key
   B. Sender uses sender's private key and receiver uses sender's public key
   C. Sender uses recipient's private key and receiver uses his public key
   D. Sender uses recipient's public key and receiver uses his private key

ANSWER: B. Public-key cryptography (also called asymmetric-key cryptography) uses a pair of keys to encrypt and decrypt content. Each user has a pair of cryptographic keys – a public encryption key and a private decryption key. The public key is widely distributed, while the private key is known only to its owner. The keys are related mathematically, but the parameters used to generate the keys are chosen so that calculating the private key from the public key is virtually impossible. The use of the keys is slightly different when authenticating content for digital signatures. With digital signatures, the sender uses his private key to digitally sign the message. The recipient uses the sender's public key, along with the message and digital signature, to confirm that the message is authentic.

123. The principle of segregation is designed to prevent which of the following security threats?

A. A user having access to a company's sensitive personal information
B. An administrator from disabling the account of another administrator
C. A single user from having complete access to perform an essential function
D. A user having access to confidential information that he does not need to know

ANSWER: C. Segregation, or separation of duties, is a classic security method to manage conflicts of interest and fraud. It restricts the amount of power held by any one individual. Generally, segregation prevents a single user from having complete access to perform an essential function, such as paying an invoice.

124. Which of the following accurately describes public-key cryptography ("PKI")?

A. Content is encrypted with a shared key and decrypted with a private key
B. Content is encrypted with a public key and decrypted with a private key
C. Content is encrypted with a public key and decrypted with a public key
D. Content is encrypted with a private key and decrypted with a private key

ANSWER: B. Public-key cryptography (also called asymmetric-key cryptography) uses a pair of keys to encrypt and decrypt content. Each user has a pair of cryptographic keys – a public encryption key and a private decryption key. The public key is widely distributed, while the private key is known only to its owner. The keys are related mathematically, but the parameters used to generate the keys are chosen so that calculating the private key from the public key is virtually impossible.

125. Which of the following is correct about authentication schemes for computer access?

   A.   Most websites rely solely on password authentication
   B.   Pass card authentication does not increase security when used in conjunction with passwords
   C.   Biometric authentication can be easily circumvented
   D.   Out of band authentication schemes are a type of one-factor authentication

ANSWER: A. Although two-factor authentication schemes drastically increase security, most websites rely solely on password authentication. Two-factor authentication is a security process in which the user provides two means of identification, one of which is typically a physical token, such as a card, and the other of which is typically something memorized, such as a security code or password. In this context, the two factors involved are sometimes referred to as something you have (e.g., a pass card) and something you know (e.g., a password).

126. Information security generally balances the risk of loss of an asset with the cost of what two factors?

   A. Intrusion detection systems and instruction prevention systems
   B. Security protection and security management
   C. Security controls and storage of the asset
   D. Replacement of the asset and storage of the asset

ANSWER: B. With respect to information security, the risk of loss is balanced with the costs of providing security to prevent loss. Security generally consists of security protection and security management (that is, the security controls and the people used to implement and manage the controls).

127. A robust information classification scheme enables what?

   A. A clearer privacy notice
   B. Test controls to detect unauthorized access
   C. Increases in computing efficiency
   D. A basis for managing access to informational assets

ANSWER: D. Information classification is an important part of managing access to informational assets. Generally information may be classified as either public, confidential, or sensitive. Depending on the classification, access should be restricted to only those persons with a need to know the information (also known as role-based access control).

128. Information security systems should be designed with what two core competing goals in mind?

A.   Minimum necessary controls and ease of use
B.   Protecting information and restricting access to the information
C.   Protecting information and providing access to the information
D.   Restricting access to information and encrypting the information

ANSWER: C. A general principle when designing an information security system is that a security professional must balance protecting information with the need to provide access to the information. These are the two primary objectives when formulating an information security system or policy.

129. Which one of the following is NOT a purpose of the APEC Privacy Framework, which was approved by APEC ministers in 2004?

A.   Improve information sharing among government agencies and regulators
B.   Establish a common set of privacy principles
C.   Encourage the use of electronic data as a means to enhance and expand business
D.   Promote the use of automated encryption mechanisms for sensitive data

ANSWER: D. The Asia-Pacific Economic Cooperation ("APEC") Privacy Framework, which is consistent with the OECD's 1980 Guidelines, has the following primary goals: (1) improve information sharing among government agencies and regulators, (2) facilitate the safe transfer of information between economies, (3) establish a common set of privacy principles, (4) encourage the use of electronic data as a means to enhance and expand business, and (5) provide technical assistance to those economies that have yet to address privacy from a regulatory or policy perspective.

130. What are the most common and important class of security control?

    A.   Preventive
    B.   Corrective
    C.   Detective
    D.   Remedial

ANSWER: A. Preventive controls are designed to protect information before a security event occurs and therefore are the most important and common type of control. Examples of preventive controls include firewalls, passwords, and encryption. Detective controls are designed to detect a security event. Examples of detective controls include security logs and intrusion detection systems. Finally, corrective controls are designed to protect information after a security event occurs. Examples of corrective controls include intrusion preventive systems that block a user after detecting suspicious activity from the user. More than one type of control may be used to protect information. For example, confidential information should be protected by several controls of varying classes. Information of lower importance, such as public information, may be protected by fewer controls (or even no controls at all).

131. The information security department at an organization should communicate information security policies to whom?

A. The information security and privacy groups responsible for the data related to the policies
B. All employees that use data related to the policies
C. Only executives and managers in the organization
D. All employees of the organization

ANSWER: D. Information security policies should be communicated to all employees and not just to the security and privacy professionals at an organization. Every employee plays a part in protecting an organization's information, even those employees without computer access. For example, a janitor may leave a door unlocked, which in turn allows an intruder to remove a computer containing personal information. Therefore, all employees should be aware of a company's information security policies.

132. What are the main sources of requirements for information security policies?

A. Organizational needs and customer demands
B. Customer requests and manager feedback
C. Relevant laws and an organization's privacy policy
D. Standards and privacy policies

ANSWER: C. The main sources of requirements for information security policies come from applicable laws, rules, and regulations, as well as from an organization's privacy policy. Although customer complaints and requests may be considered when developing an information security policy, they are not a main source of requirements and inclusion would be optional.

133. What is the step of information security incident management after containment and analysis of a security breach?

    A.   Discovery
    B.   Prevention
    C.   Eradication
    D.   Notification

ANSWER: D. When an information security incident occurs, an organization must know how to appropriately respond. The basic incident management and response process includes (1) incident discovery, (2) containment and analysis, (3) notification, and (4) eradication and prevention.

134. Which of the following is a standard formula for assessing information technology risk?

    A.   Risk = Threat x Vulnerability x Expected Loss
    B.   Risk = Control / Threat x Vulnerability
    C.   Risk = Threat + Vulnerability − Expected Loss
    D.   Risk = Threat x Vulnerability / Control

ANSWER: A. As indicated by the correct formula, the risk associated with an organization's information technology is directly related to three parameters: (1) threats, (2) vulnerabilities, and (3) expected loss.

Threats are circumstances that may cause an undesirable event, such as a data breach. Vulnerabilities are weaknesses in an organization's information systems, policies, or procedures. When a threat exploits some vulnerability, a security event that causes risk occurs. The amount of the risk for a particular security event is equal to the probability of the event occurring times the expected loss associated with the event. Answers B, C, and D provide incorrect formulations of risk.

135. In addition to threats and vulnerabilities, what other factor should be considered when evaluating risk?

    A.   Controls
    B.   Expected Loss
    C.   Technical safeguards
    D.   Likelihood of system failure

ANSWER: B. The risk associated with an organization's information technology is directly related to three parameters: (1) threats, (2) vulnerabilities, and (3) expected loss.

136. Which of the following is NOT a major source of information security requirements for an organization?

    A.   Legal and regulatory obligations
    B.   The organization's privacy policy
    C.   Contractual obligations
    D.   Customer complaints and evaluations

ANSWER: D. Legal, regulatory, and contractual obligations are all primary sources of information security requirements for an organization. An organization's privacy policy is also another major source of security requirements. Customer complaints and evaluations, on the other hand, are not a primary source. Addressing customer complaints would typically be optional and not a requirement.

137. In accordance with information security best practices, which employees of an organization are responsible for information security?

A.   Information security personnel
B.   All managers
C.   All employees
D.   The executive team

ANSWER: C. While information security personnel can perform a wide range of tasks related to information security at an organization, ultimately all employees are responsible for ensuring information security. Accordingly, all employees should be trained in information handling best practices.

138. Which of the following is one of the first steps when establishing an information security program?

A.   Monitor the security program
B.   Identify and evaluate risks
C.   Define the security policy
D.   Review complaints and evaluations

ANSWER: C. Generally, an information security program should be established by (1) defining the security policy and security management system; (2) identifying and evaluating risks, (3) selecting appropriate controls to address the identified risks, (4) obtaining management approval of the program, and (5) monitoring and reviewing compliance with the program.

139. What type of log should record a device driver that fails to load properly?

A.   Security log
B.   System log
C.   Application log
D.   Device log

ANSWER: B. A system log contains events that are logged by the operating system and its components, such as device drivers. An application log records events that are triggered by the applications used on a computer system, such as a database application. Events that are written to the application log are determined by the developers of the software program, not the operating system. A security log is used to track security-related information on a computer system. The security log typically contains a record of login/logout activity and other security-related events specified by the system's audit policy.

140. In which country is express authorization from the data protection authority required for the automatic processing of biometric data?

A. France
B. Australia
C. Canada
D. United States

ANSWER: A. In France, express authorization must be obtained from the Commission Nationale de l'informatique et des Libertés (the "CNIL") before the automatic processing of biometric data.

141. Which of the following is NOT a principle set forth in the Guidelines on the Protection of Privacy and Transborder Flows of Personal Data adopted by the Organization for Economic Cooperation and Development in 1980 ("OECD Guidelines")?

A. Data Quality
B. Collection Limitation
C. Openness
D. Adequate Protection

ANSWER: D. The eight principles contained in the OECD Guidelines are: (1) collection limitation principles, (2) data quality principle, (3) purpose specification principle, (4) use limitation principle, (5) security safeguards principle, (6) openness principle, (7) individual participation principle, and (8) accountability principle. Adequate protection is not one of the principles.

142. What are the primary goals EU Data Protection Directive?

   A.   Reduce piracy and discourage international transfers of personal information
   B.   Safeguard the fundamental right of privacy and enable the free flow of personal information among member states
   C.   Encourage international transfers of personal information and safeguard Internet users
   D.   Safeguard the fundamental right of privacy and protect children from the illegal collection of personal information

ANSWER: B. Article 3 of the EU Data Protection Directive indicates that its main goals are (1) safeguarding the fundamental right of privacy and (2) enabling the free flow of personal information among member states.

143. Who is responsible for protecting informational assets at an organization?

   A.   All employees, vendors, and consultants
   B.   Employees in the information security department
   C.   Managers
   D.   The chief executive officer

ANSWER: A. While information security personnel can perform a wide range of tasks related to information security at an organization, it is every employees' responsibility to protect informational assets. Information security is ultimately about people. Vendors and consultants should always be informed of information security policies and procedures if they are given access to information.

144. Which of the following is NOT a privacy principle of the Safe Harbor program developed by the Department of Commerce in consultation with the European Commission?

A. Notice
B. Choice
C. Access
D. Mutual respect

ANSWER: D. The European Union ("EU") Data Protection Directive prohibits the transfer of personal data to non-European Union countries that do not meet the European Union (EU) "adequacy" standard for privacy protection. While the United States and the EU share the goal of enhancing privacy protection for their citizens, the United States takes a different approach to privacy than that of the EU. The U.S. Department of Commerce in consultation with the European Commission developed the Safe Harbor framework to bridge these differences in approach and provide a streamlined means for U.S. organizations to comply with the Directive. Organizations desiring to join the program must comply with the seven Safe Harbor privacy principles, which are (1) notice, (2) choice, (3) onward transfer to third parties, (4) access, (5) security, (6) data integrity, and (7) enforcement. Mutual respect is not one of the principles.

145. Which of the following is NOT a principle of privacy by design?

A.   Visibility and transparency
B.   Privacy as the default setting
C.   Equal treatment of data
D.   End-to-end security

ANSWER: C. The Information and Privacy Commissioner of Ontario, Canada developed the privacy by design framework in the 1990s. It includes the following seven principles: (1) Proactive not Reactive; Preventative not Remedial; (2) Privacy as the Default Setting; (3) Privacy Embedded into Design, (4) Full Functionality — Positive-Sum, not Zero-Sum; (5) End-to-End Security — Full Lifecycle Protection; (6)Visibility and Transparency — Keep it Open; and (7) Respect for User Privacy — Keep it User-Centric. Equal treatment of data is not one of the principles in privacy by design.

146. Which of the following accurately describes an organization's ability to monitor its employees in the EU?

A.   Employee monitoring is never permitted
B.   Employee monitoring is permitted only within common area that are owned by the organization
C.   Employee monitoring is permitted only with the express verbal consent of the employee
D.   Personal data processed in connection with the monitoring must be adequate, relevant, and not excessive

ANSWER: D. Once an employer decides to monitor an employee, the Article 29 Working Party suggests that the organization follow the following seven basic principles: (1) an employer must determine whether the monitoring is absolutely necessary for the specified purpose, (2) data collected through the monitoring must respond to a "specified, explicit and legitimate" purpose and cannot be processed for a different purpose, (3) the employer must provide clear and open notice to employees about the monitoring, (4) employers may monitor only to safeguard their legitimate interests, while not violating an employee's fundamental rights, (5) personal data processed in connection with the monitoring must be adequate, relevant, and not excessive, (6) personal data must be updated and retained only for the period deemed necessary for the purpose to be achieved, and (7) the employer must implement all appropriate technical and organizational measures to ensure that any personal data is protected from alteration, unauthorized access, and misuse.

147. Which of the following is NOT an exception to the EU Data Protection Directive's requirement that transfers of personal data may only be made to countries which ensure an adequate level of protection?

A.   The transfer complies with all applicable laws of the receiving country
B.   The transfer is necessary for the performance of a contract between the data subject and the controller
C.   The transfer is necessary in order to protect the vital interests of the data subject
D.   The transfer is necessary or legally required on important public interest grounds

ANSWER: A. Article 26(1) of the EU Data Protection Directive states that transfers of personal data to a third country which do not ensure an adequate level of protection may take place if the data subject has "given his consent unambiguously to the proposed transfer." Other exceptions include: (1) the transfer is necessary for the performance of a contract between the data subject and the controller, (2) the transfer is necessary for the conclusion or performance of a contract concluded in the interest of the data subject, (3) the transfer is necessary or legally required on important public interest grounds, and (4) the transfer is necessary in order to protect the vital interests of the data subject. Answers B, C, and D set forth valid exceptions.

148. Which of the following may be classified as a deceptive trade practice by the FTC?

A. A website's privacy notice clearly states that it will not encrypt sensitive personal information, and the website does not, in fact, encrypt the data

B. An organization promises to honor opt-out requests within 10 days but fails to honor opt-out requests

C. A rogue employee steals credit card information even though the organization took reasonable precautions to protect the credit card information

D. A bank does not comply with a regulation prohibiting the bank from revealing information about its customers

ANSWER: B. If an organization fails to comply with its privacy notice, it may be held liable by the FTC for a deceptive trade practice under Section 5 of the FTC Act, which prohibits "unfair or deceptive acts or practices in or affecting commerce." When companies state that they will safeguard personal information, the FTC can and does take law enforcement action to make sure that companies live up to these promises. A violation of a promise made in a privacy notice is an example of a deceptive trade practice. Answer A would be an example of an unfair trade practice. The organization is not being deceptive, but the potential harm caused by the website's failure to encrypt sensitive data clearly outweighs the cost of providing encryption, a commonplace and inexpensive security control. Answer C would not be a deceptive trade practice because the organization had reasonable security measures, and the employee simply committed a crime, an unforeseeable event. Answer

D is incorrect because the FTC has no jurisdiction over banks and common carriers, which are under the supervision of other governmental agencies.

149. Which of the following is NOT a common category of information used when developing information security controls?

A.   Public
B.   Sensitive
C.   Confidential
D.   Personal

ANSWER: D. The most common information classification scheme divides information into three categories: (1) public information, (2) sensitive information, and (3) confidential information. Public information by its very nature is designed to be shared broadly, without restriction. Examples of public information include marketing material, press releases, and regulatory reports submitted to government agencies. Sensitive information is considered internal and should not be released outside an organization. Examples of sensitive information include business plans, financial data, and documents reflecting corporate strategy. Confidential information is generally intended for a very specific purpose and should not be disclosed to anyone without a demonstrated need to know. Examples of confidential information include employee bank account information, Social Security numbers, and login credentials (e.g., username and password).

150. What is the first step of information security incident management?

A. Prevention
B. Containment
C. Analysis
D. Discovery

ANSWER: D. When an information security incident occurs, an organization must know how to appropriately respond. The basic incident management and response process includes (1) incident discovery, (2) containment and analysis, (3) notification, and (4) eradication and prevention.

About the CIPP/US Exam

The Certified Information Privacy Professional/United States ("CIPP/US") examination is one of seven specialty exams administered by the International Association of Privacy Professionals ("IAPP"). The exam covers U.S. privacy laws and regulations, as well as the requirements for transferring personal information into and out of the United States.

To receive a certification from the IAPP, a candidate must successfully pass the Certification Foundation exam and one other specialty exam, including the CIPP/US, CIPP/C, CIPP/E, CIPP/G, CIPP/IT, CIPM, and CIPT.

The CIPP/US exam is an 80 minute, 72 item, objective (that is, multiple-choice) test. There are no essay questions, and each correct answer is worth one point. The exam includes 60 scored items and 12 non-scored, trial items. You will not know which questions are scored when taking the exam, and therefore you should treat all questions as if they are scored.

Also, you are not penalized for incorrect answers. Therefore, a general exam taking strategy is to answer every question on the exam, even those you are unsure of. Eliminate obviously incorrect answers and then choose the best answer remaining. Do not leave any questions unanswered.

Lastly, on a more personal note, be sure to give yourself adequate time to prepare for the examination. This guide is quite lengthy, and you will need several weeks (at a minimum) to work through all of the material. Take your time and absorb the material. You will not obtain a firm grasp of the information contained in this guide by simply skimming it. Carefully read the sample questions and detailed answers provided at the end of this guide. You will likely see dozens of questions on your exam that test the same subject matter as our sample questions. If you answer these questions correctly, you are well on your way to becoming a certified privacy professional.

Good Luck!

Chapter 5: Overview of U.S. Privacy Principles

This chapter addresses common themes and principles of information privacy in the United States. You should expect anywhere from 15 to 20 questions on your examination testing subject matter covered in this chapter.

A. Glossary Terms

It is important that you thoroughly understand the framework in the United States for protecting an individual's privacy. Therefore, you should carefully read the definitions provided in the glossary for the important terms listed below. The glossary is located at:

http://www.cippexam.com/glossary

Glossary Terms: Accountability, APEC Privacy Principles, Behavioral Advertising, Binding Corporate Rules, Case Law, Choice, Commercial Activity, Common Law, Confirmed Opt In, Consent Decree, Data Classification, Deceptive Trade Practices, Do Not Track, Encryption, EU-U.S. Safe Harbor Agreement, Global Privacy Enforcement Network, Jurisdiction, Negligence, OECD Guidelines, Omnibus Laws, Online Behavioral Advertising, Opt-In, Opt-Out, Organization for Economic Cooperation and Development, PCI Data Security Standard, Preemption, Privacy Act of 1974, Privacy by Design, Privacy Notice, Privacy Policy, Private Right of Action, Seal Programs, Self-Regulation Model, Smart Grid, Unfair Trade Practices.

B. Basic Legal Principles in the United States

Understanding the legal framework in the United States is an important part of understanding privacy. The U.S. Constitution is the supreme law of the United States. It separates the United States government into three main powers, or branches. The legislative branch makes the laws, the executive branch enforces the laws, and the judicial branch evaluates and interprets the laws. The purpose of the separate branches is to create a separation of powers, thereby ensuring no one person has too much control of the government.

Figure 10 illustrates the three branches and provides other important information about each branch.

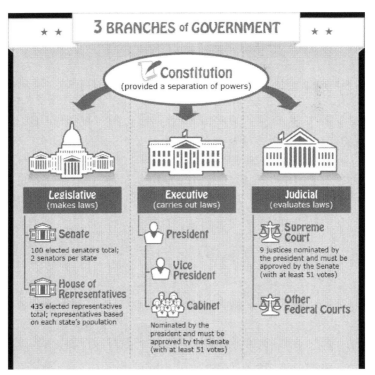

Figure 10: Branches of the U.S. Government

When making laws, the Senate and House of Representatives (collectively referred to as "Congress") may authorize specific federal agencies to create regulations that implement the laws. For example, Congress has partially delegated its duty to implement and enforce privacy laws to the U.S. Federal Trade Commission ("FTC"). The FTC is the main federal agency in the United States responsible for implementing and enforcing privacy laws in the United States.

C. Primary Sources and Types of American Law

American law is derived from various sources. The legislative branch is responsible for making statutory laws (a form of written law), but other types and sources of law also exist.

For example, the U.S. Constitution is the supreme law of the United States and contains many provisions relevant to privacy, such as the Fourth Amendment's prohibition against unreasonable searches and seizures. Although the U.S. Constitution does not provide an explicit right to privacy, several state constitutions (most notably California's) do set forth an explicit right to privacy.

The four main types of laws in the United States are:

1. Constitutional law: The U.S. and state constitutions are a primary source of law in America. As previously discussed, state constitutions may afford greater protection than the U.S. Constitution in important areas, such as privacy.

2. <u>Statutory law</u>: Legislatures create statutes, a form of written law. Statutes may originate with the national legislature (Congress), state legislatures, or local municipalities. Statutory laws are subordinate to the higher constitutional laws of the land. In addition, federal laws enacted by Congress may supersede state laws that regulate the same or a similar area (a doctrine called "preemption").

3. <u>Administrative law</u>: Administrative and regulatory agencies, such as the Federal Trade Commission ("FTC") and Federal Communication Commission ("FCC"), promulgate rules and regulations that form a body of administrative law. These rules and regulations are published in the Federal Register, the official journal of the federal government of the United States.

4. <u>Common law</u>: This type of law is developed by judges through decisions of courts (called "case law") and similar tribunals, as opposed to statutes adopted through the legislative process or regulations issued by the executive branch. Common law is generally based on societal customs and expectations.

Figure 11 on the following page illustrates the various types of American law.

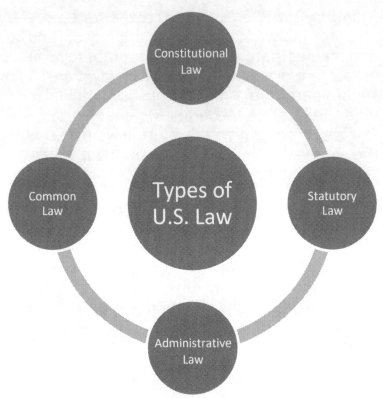

Figure 11: Types of U.S. Law

D. Overview of U.S. Privacy Principles

The United States takes a sectoral approach to information privacy. In other words, specific laws protect privacy rights for a given sector of industry, rather than a general, comprehensive data protection law applicable to all sectors (as is found in Europe).

For example, the Health Insurance Portability and Accountability Act ("HIPAA") protects privacy interests in the healthcare industry by defining policies, procedures and guidelines to which covered entities must adhere in order to maintain the privacy and security of individually identifiable protected health information ("PHI"). Therefore, HIPAA is a federal privacy law that regulates a specific industry – the healthcare industry.

In 2012, the Obama administration released a report titled "Consumer Data Privacy in a Networked World: A Framework for Protecting Privacy and Promoting Innovation in the Global Economy." In this report, President Obama summarized the privacy framework in the United States as follows:

> The consumer data privacy framework in the United States is, in fact, strong. This framework rests on fundamental privacy values, flexible and adaptable common law protections and consumer protection statutes, Federal Trade Commission (FTC) enforcement, and policy development that involves a broad array of stakeholders. This framework has encouraged not only social and economic innovations based on the Internet but also vibrant discussions of how to protect privacy in a networked society involving civil society, industry, academia, and the government.

In other words, information privacy is an important right in the United States and is protected by an interrelated network of industry-specific laws and enforcement agencies. Therefore, to gain a full understanding of information privacy in the United States, you must have a strong working knowledge of the various laws regulating privacy, as well as the regime for enforcing these laws. Section G of this chapter discusses the FTC's dominant role in enforcing privacy laws, while the remaining chapters in this book address industry-specific laws that regulate both private and public sectors in the United States.

E. Privacy Policies and Notices

Although many people use the terms "privacy policy" and "privacy notice" interchangeably, these terms actually represent two distinct privacy statements.

A privacy policy is an internal statement that describes an organization's information handling practices and procedures. It is directed towards the employees and agents of the organization.

A privacy notice, on the other hand, is an external statement that is directed to an organization's prospective and actual customers or users. It generally describes how the organization will process personal information it receives from its users. The privacy notice also typically describes the options that users have with respect to the organization's processing of their personal information (for example, the opportunity to "opt out"). An organization will commonly use its privacy policy as a privacy notice. For example, an organization may publish its privacy notice on its website and rebrand the notice as a privacy policy.

The distinction between a privacy policy and a privacy notice is often tested on the Certification Foundation and CIPP/US exams. In addition, many incorrect answers on the exam will use these terms incorrectly. For example, if an answer choice implies that a privacy policy is used as an external statement to inform customers about an organization's privacy practices, it is not likely the correct answer.

On the exam, "privacy policy" and "privacy notice" represent two distinct privacy statements. Again, a privacy policy is an internal statement, while a privacy notice is an external statement. This makes intuitive sense because policies are generally internal operating documents, while notices are typically external announcements. You should keep this distinction in mind during your exam.

F. Types of Choices and Consent

There are two fundamental types of choices and consent that an organization may provide to, or receive from, a data subject. The first is called "opt-in" consent, and the second is called "opt-out" consent.

Opt-in consent occurs when users (commonly referred to as "data subjects") affirmatively and explicitly indicate their desire to have their data processed by an organization (commonly referred to as the "data processor"). For example, when a data subject expressly tells a data processor that certain specified types of processing are allowed, that data subject is opting in to the specified processing. Opt-in consent is sometimes referred to as affirmative consent.

Opt-out consent, on the other hand, is when data subjects implicitly consent by not indicating their disapproval of the requested processing. For example, if a data processor tells data subjects that their data will be processed in a particular way unless the processor is notified within ten days, the processor is providing the data subjects with the opportunity to opt out.

A good way to remember the difference between opt-in and opt-out consent is to consider what happens to a data subject's information if no action is taken. With opt-in consent, information is excluded from processing if the data subject does not act. With opt-out consent, information is <u>included</u> in processing if the data subject does not act.

In connection with online data processing, opt-in and opt-out consent can be illustrated with the web form shown in Figure 12.

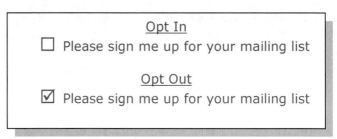

Figure 12: Opt In and Opt Out Illustration

With opt-in consent, the data subject must affirmatively check the box in order to join the mailing list. The default action is that the data subject will not be added to the mailing list. With opt-out consent, the box is pre-checked, and the data subject will join the mailing list unless the box is unselected. Thus, the default action is inclusion on the mailing list.

As will be described later in this guide, some types of processing will require affirmative opting in by a data subject, while other types of processing require only opt-out consent. Opt-in consent is generally reserved for more intrusive processing, such as the transfer of sensitive personal information to third parties, while opt-out consent is appropriate for less intrusive forms of processing, such as the sending of commercial emails to a recipient when an existing business relationship exists.

An organization is not required to provide a data subject with choice under all circumstances. Specifically, companies do not need to provide a choice before collecting and using consumer data for practices that are consistent with the context of the transaction or the company's relationship with the consumer.

For example, when ordering a product through an online retailer, the purchaser understands that the retailer may share both the purchaser's address with the shipping company and credit card information with the billing agent. In essence, the purchaser has implicitly consented to the sharing of personal information by virtue of entering into the transaction. Therefore, in these circumstances, an organization does not need to provide a form of choice when processing personal information.

G. The FTC's Role in Privacy Enforcement

As previously mentioned, the U.S. Federal Trade Commission ("FTC") is the primary agency responsible for enforcing privacy laws in the United States. The FTC is an independent agency of the federal government established in 1914 by the Federal Trade Commission Act. Although the FTC was originally founded to enforce antitrust laws, today its primary mission is the promotion of consumer protection and the elimination and prevention of anticompetitive business practices, such as coercive monopolies.

Section 5 of the Federal Trade Commission Act grants the FTC power to investigate and prevent (1) unfair trade practices and (2) deceptive trade practices. The legal standards for unfairness and deception are independent of each other. Depending on the facts, an act or practice may be unfair, deceptive, or both.

An act or practice is <u>unfair</u> when it (1) causes or is likely to cause substantial injury to consumers; (2) cannot be reasonably avoided by consumers; and (3) is not outweighed by countervailing benefits to consumers or to competition. Public policy, as established by statute, regulation, or judicial decisions, may be considered with all other evidence in determining whether an act or practice is unfair.

An act or practice is <u>deceptive</u> when (1) a representation, omission, or practice misleads or is likely to mislead the consumer; (2) a consumer's interpretation of the representation, omission, or practice is considered reasonable under the circumstances; and (3) the misleading representation, omission, or practice is material.

Figure 13 summarizes the standards for both deceptive and unfair trade practices. Before taking your exam, you should familiarize yourself with both of these important standards.

Deceptive Trade Practice	Unfair Trade Practice
A representation, omission, or practice misleads or is likely to mislead the consumer; A consumer's interpretation of the representation, omission, or practice is considered reasonable under the circumstances; and The misleading representation, omission, or practice is material	Causes or is likely to cause substantial injury to consumers; Cannot be reasonably avoided by consumers; and Is not outweighed by countervailing benefits to consumers or to competition

Figure 13: Deceptive and Unfair Trade Practices

The FTC's enforcement power applies broadly to all persons or entities engaged in commerce <u>except for banks</u>. Banks are regulated by various other agencies, including the Office of the Comptroller of the Currency, the Federal Reserve Board, the Federal Deposit Insurance Corporation ("FDIC"), Office of Thrift Supervision, and the National Credit Union Administration.

When the FTC believes that a person or company has committed an unfair or deceptive trade practice, it starts an investigation of the practice. Following the investigation, the FTC may initiate an enforcement action against the person or organization if it has "reason to believe" that the law is being, or has been, violated. An enforcement action begins with the FTC issuing a complaint setting forth its charges.

After a complaint is issued, the entity being charged generally has two options for responding. First, it may elect to settle the charges by entering into a <u>consent decree</u>. Second, the entity may contest the charges and request an <u>administrative trial</u> before an administrative law judge ("ALJ").

A consent decree is a formal document stating specific steps the entity needs to perform to rectify the violation. It sometimes includes a specific monetary fine. When entering into a consent decree, the charged entity does not admit fault or liability. This is an important aspect of a consent decree: the alleged violator does not admit to any wrongdoing, which is beneficial to the charged entity because the decree cannot be used as evidence of fault in any other civil action that may be brought by those harmed by the unfair or deceptive practice. Most organizations therefore choose to enter into a consent decree because they avoid the time, expense, and negative publicity associated with a prolonged trial and obviate the detrimental effects of admitting fault.

H. Information Management Principles

For privacy purposes, all information can be classified as either (1) personal information or (2) non-personal information. Personal information is any information (both paper and electronic records) that relates to or describes an <u>identified or identifiable individual</u>.

Accordingly, information about a corporation is generally not considered personal information because it does not relate to an individual. In the United States, the term "personally identifiable information" (or "PII") is typically used to refer to personal information.

There are many benefits and risks associated with processing personal information. An obvious benefit is the ability to create a more personalized experience for your users. For example, an online dating service may use personal information to help match its users based on age, gender, and personal preferences. Therefore, processing personal information may result in a tailored experience that is mutually beneficial to both the data processor and the data subject.

Many companies that process personal information develop an <u>information management program</u> to balance the risks and benefits of handling personal information. When developing an information management program, the following four risks should be evaluated and considered:

1. Legal Risk: An organization should comply with all applicable local, state, and federal laws, rules and regulations. If it does not, the organization is subject to legal risk for its failure to comply and the harm it causes to others. Legal risk also occurs when an organization does not comply with its privacy policy and other obligations it has made. When implementing a privacy program, an organization should minimize its legal risk by ensuring that it is in compliance with its own privacy policy, as well as all applicable local, state, and federal laws.

2. Operational Risk: Inadequate or failed internal processes and systems may result in actual loss for an organization in terms of wasted resources. Therefore, when implementing a privacy program, an organization should ensure that its program is cost-effective and administratively efficient, thereby ensuring the operational risk associated with the program is within accepted tolerances.

3. Reputational Risk: An organization's reputation is arguably one of its most important assets. Consumer confidence and trust can have a direct and profound effect on an organization's revenue. Accordingly, when implementing a privacy policy, an organization should ensure that it follows through on the promises contained in its privacy policy, thereby building and maintaining its reputation and relationship with the consumer.

4. Investment Risk: Building and implementing a privacy program requires the investment of resources, both in terms of personnel and information technology. As with any investment, an organization should ensure that it receives an

adequate return on its investment by constantly monitoring the costs associated with the program.

Figure 14 illustrates the various types of risk that should be considered when developing an information management program.

Figure 14: Types of Information Management Risk

Once the various risks have been evaluated and quantified, these risks should be balanced with the anticipated benefits associated with the processing of personal information. This balancing analysis will assist the company in rendering an informed decision regarding whether or not to process specific types of personal information in specified ways.

At a high level, an information management program is simply a tool that provides a framework for making well-reasoned decisions regarding the company's processing of personal information. The program also helps an organization comply with its various legal obligations associated with the handling of personal information.

Various stakeholders throughout the organization should participate in the development and design of an information management program. In addition, it is important to periodically reevaluate and update the program to ensure that it is adequately capturing the anticipated risks and benefits associated with the processing of personal information. This is especially true when an organization decides to substantively change the way it uses or processes personal information.

Chapter 6: U.S. Privacy Laws Regulating the Private Sector

This chapter addresses the major privacy laws that regulate the private sector in the United States. You should expect anywhere from 14 to 18 questions on your examination directed to subject matter from this chapter.

A. Glossary Terms

Your exam will contain a relatively high number of questions testing material from this chapter. Therefore, it is important that you read the definitions provided in the glossary for the important terms listed below. The glossary is located at:

http://www.cippexam.com/glossary

Glossary Terms: Adverse Action, Bank Secrecy Act, Children's Online Privacy Protection Act of 2000, Commercial Electronic Message, Communications Privacy, Consumer Reporting Agency, Data Elements, Deidentification, Digital Signature, Electronic Health Record, Established Business Relationship, Fair Credit Reporting Act, Gramm-Leach-Bliley Act, Health Information Technology for Economic and Clinical Health Act, Health Insurance Portability and Accountability Act, Medical Information, Minimum Necessary Requirement, Non-Public Personal Information, Privacy Rule, Protected Health Information, USA-PATRIOT Act, Voice Over Internet Protocol.

B. Privacy Laws Regulating the Healthcare Industry

Two important federal laws regulate the processing of personal information in the healthcare industry: (1) the Health Insurance Portability and Accountability Act ("HIPAA") and (2) the Genetic Information Nondiscrimination Act ("GINA"). Each of these laws is discussed below in turn.

3. Health Insurance Portability and Accountability Act ("HIPAA")

HIPAA was enacted in 1996 to define policies, procedures, and guidelines that <u>covered entities</u> must follow for maintaining the privacy and security of individually identifiable protected health information ("PHI"). PHI includes all information that relates to (1) the past, present, or future physical or mental health or condition of an individual; (2) the provision of health care to an individual; or (3) the past, present, or future payment for the provision of health care to an individual.

Covered entities generally include healthcare clearinghouses, employer sponsored health plans, health insurers, and healthcare providers.

During your exam, it is important to remember which entities are regulated by HIPAA. Again, HIPAA only applies to healthcare clearinghouses, employer sponsored health plans, health insurers, and healthcare providers. For example, both public and private hospitals are clearly covered by HIPAA because they are healthcare providers. However, other entities that sell health-related information, such as an online retailer of medical books, are not covered entities even though a customer's purchase history may reveal a medical condition that the customer possesses.

As directed by Title II of HIPAA, the Department of Health and Human Services ("HHS") has promulgated two important rules to address the handling of PHI: (1) the Privacy Rule and (2) the Security Rule.

Under the Privacy Rule, covered entities may only disclose PHI to facilitate treatment, payment, or healthcare operations without a patient's express written authorization. Any other disclosure of PHI requires the covered entity to obtain written authorization from the data subject for the disclosure. In addition, when a covered entity discloses PHI, it must make reasonable efforts to disclose only the minimum necessary information required to achieve its purpose.

The Privacy Rule does not apply to information that has been "de-identified." There are two methods expressly provided in the Privacy Rule for de-identifying information. First, all specific identifiers may be removed from the information. Second, a qualified statistical expert may draft an opinion that the risk of identifying an individual associated with the information is very small under the circumstances. If information has been de-identified, the Privacy Rule does not apply to the information, and covered entities may freely disclose the information to third-parties and use the information for other purposes, including research.

While the Privacy Rule pertains to all forms of PHI, including both paper and electronic records, the Security Rule covers only electronic Protected Health Information ("ePHI"). In accordance with the Security

Rule, covered entities must implement three types of security safeguards to protect ePHI:
(1) administrative, (2) physical, and (3) technical. For each type of safeguard, the Security Rule identifies various security standards, and for each standard, it provides both required and addressable implementation specifications.

For your exam, it is important to remember that the Security Rule applies only to electronics records, while the Privacy Rule covers all heath records regardless of form.

In 2009, the Health Information Technology for Economic and Clinical Health ("HITECH") Act expanded HIPAA's Privacy and Security Rules to directly regulate "business associates" of covered entities. Business associates are persons or organization that process PHI on behalf of a covered entity. Previously, covered entities were only required to enter into a contractual agreement with business associates to ensure the privacy and security of protected health information. Today, HIPAA applies directly to both covered entities and their business associates in accordance with the HITECH Act.

The HITECH Act also sets forth specific rules that covered entities and their business associates must adhere to when there is a data breach involving unsecured PHI. Specifically, when unsecured PHI has been (or is reasonably believed to have been) accessed, acquired, or disclosed as a result of a data breach, the covered entity must provide notice to each affected individual and the Department of Health and Human Services ("HHS"). The notification must occur within 60 calendar days after the discovery of the breach. Business associates of a covered entity are also required to notify the covered entity when a data breach occurs. When the data breach affects 500 or more individuals in the same state or jurisdiction, the covered entity must also notify the media and provide immediate notification of the breach to the HSS.

During your exam, it is important to remember that the breach notification regulations apply only to <u>unsecured</u> health information. Therefore, the notification requirement does not apply to entities that secure health information, for example, through encryption.

4. Genetic Information Nondiscrimination Act ("GINA")

The Genetic Information Nondiscrimination Act ("GINA") was enacted in 2008. GINA protects individuals against discrimination based on their genetic information in health coverage and in employment. GINA is divided into two sections, or Titles. Title I of GINA prohibits discrimination based on genetic information in health coverage. Title II of GINA prohibits discrimination based on genetic information in employment.

Title I makes it illegal for health insurance providers to use or require genetic information to make decisions about a person's insurance eligibility or coverage.

Title II makes it illegal for employers to use a person's genetic information when making decisions about hiring, promotion, and several other terms of employment.

One of the primary goals of GINA is to encourage individuals to obtain genetic screenings without fear of discrimination based on the results of the screening.

GINA is further discussed in Chapter 4 of this guide, which addresses workplace privacy.

C. Privacy Laws Regulating the Financial Industry

Four important federal laws regulate the processing of personal information in the financial industry: (1) the Fair Credit Reporting Act ("FCRA"), (2) the Gramm-Leach-Bliley Act ("GLBA"), (3) the Dodd-Frank Wall Street Reform and Consumer Protection Act ("Dodd-Frank Act"); and (4) the Bank Secrecy Act. Each of these important federal laws is discussed below in turn.

1. Fair Credit Reporting Act ("FCRA")

The Fair Credit Reporting Act ("FCRA") was originally enacted in 1970 and then subsequently updated by the Fair and Accurate Credit Transactions Act of 2003 ("FACTA"). The FCRA primarily applies to (1) consumer reporting agencies (e.g., Experian, TransUnion, and Equifax) and (2) users of consumer reports (that is, the person or entity requesting the consumer report). The main purposes of the FCRA are to increase the accuracy and fairness of credit reporting and to limit the use of consumer reports to permissible purposes, such as for employment and the underwriting of insurance.

As an initial matter, it is important to understand how the FCRA defines consumer reporting agencies and consumer reports, which are the two primary objects used by the FCRA to regulate the financial industry.

A consumer reporting agency is any entity that regularly engages in the practice of assembling or evaluating consumer credit information or other information on consumers for the purpose of furnishing consumer reports to third parties.

A <u>consumer report</u> is any written, oral, or auxiliary communication of any information by a consumer reporting agency bearing on a consumer's credit worthiness, credit standing, credit capacity, character, general reputation, personal characteristics, or mode of living which is used in establishing the consumer's eligibility for (A) credit or insurance; (B) employment purposes; or (C) a license.

In addition to consumer reports, the FCRA also regulates the use of a special class of reports called "investigative consumer reports." Investigative consumer reports are consumer reports in which information on a consumer's character, general reputation, personal characteristics, or mode of living is obtained through personal interviews with persons having knowledge of the consumer, including neighbors, friends, or associates of the consumer.

In accordance with the FCRA, consumer reporting agencies have several responsibilities. First, consumer reporting agencies may only furnish consumer reports to persons having a <u>permissible purpose</u>. Permissible purposes include use in connection with (1) credit transactions, (2) employment purposes, (3) underwriting of insurance, and (4) eligibility for a license. A consumer reporting agency may also furnish consumer reports in accordance with the written instructions of the consumer to whom the report relates. Accordingly, the express written instructions of the consumer constitute a permissible purpose under the FCRA.

Second, consumer reporting agencies must ensure that their consumer reports do not contain prohibited information. Prohibited information includes bankruptcies more than ten years old and other adverse information, such as accounts placed in collection that are more than seven years old.

Third, consumer reporting agencies must follow reasonable procedures to assure the accuracy of information contained in consumer reports.

Fourth, every consumer reporting agency must, upon request, clearly and accurately disclose to the consumer all information in the consumer's file at the time of the request. In addition, consumer reporting agencies must disclose every person that procured the consumer's report for employment purposes within the last two years (and for all other purposes within the last year).

Fifth, if the completeness or accuracy of any information contained in a consumer's file at a consumer reporting agency is disputed by the consumer, and the consumer notifies the agency of the dispute, the agency must, free of charge, conduct a reasonable reinvestigation to determine whether the disputed information is accurate. Generally, the consumer reporting agency has thirty days to investigate the dispute and remove or correct the disputed item.

Lastly, all nationwide consumer reporting agencies must annually provide a free copy of a consumer's report upon request of the consumer. Additionally, if the consumer receives an adverse decision based on his or her consumer report, the consumer may request a free copy of his report within sixty days of receiving the adverse notice.

Users of consumer reports also have several responsibilities. First, users of consumer reports must certify to the consumer reporting agency their permissible purpose and also certify that the information contained in the consumer report will not be used for any other purpose.

Second, if a user of a consumer report takes any adverse action with respect to any consumer that is based in whole or in part on any information contained in a consumer report, the user must (1) provide notice of the adverse action to the consumer, (2) disclose the name, address, and telephone number of the consumer reporting agency furnishing the information to the user, and (3) notify the consumer about his right to request a free copy of his consumer report from the consumer reporting agency if the request is made within sixty days of receiving the adverse notice.

Finally, before furnishing a consumer report <u>for employment purposes</u>, a consumer reporting agency must receive certification from the user of the report that the user has written authorization from the consumer to obtain the report.

With respect to investigative consumer reports, a person may not obtain an investigative consumer report on any consumer unless (1) the consumer is notified within three days after the report was requested and (2) a certification of the notification is provided to the consumer reporting agency. A consumer may, within a reasonable period of time after receiving the notification, request a complete and accurate disclosure of the nature and scope of the investigation.

Consumers that believe that the FCRA has been violated may enforce many of its provisions through a private right of action in federal court. Any person who willfully fails to comply with any requirement imposed by the FCRA with respect to any consumer is liable to that consumer in an amount up to $1,000. In addition, a successful claimant is entitled to reasonable attorney's fees and costs. A court may also award punitive damages. State attorneys general and the FTC also have enforcement power.

The Fair and Accurate Credit Transactions Act of 2003 ("FACTA") amended the FCRA to include a "Red Flags" Rule designed to combat identify theft. Identity theft refers to fraud committed or attempted using the identifying information of another person without authority. The Red Flags Rule requires "creditors" and "financial institutions" to address the risk of identity theft by developing and implementing written identity theft prevention programs to help identify, detect, and respond to patterns, practices, or specific activities – known as red flags – that could indicate identity theft.

In addition to the Red Flags Rule, FACTA also sets forth a Disposal Rule that went into effect in 2005. In accordance with the Disposal Rule, any business or individual who uses a consumer report for a business purpose must ensure the proper disposal of information in the consumer report to protect against "unauthorized access to or use of the information."

The standard for the proper disposal of information derived from a consumer report is flexible and allows the organizations and individuals covered by the

Disposal Rule to determine what measures are reasonable based on the sensitivity of the information, the costs and benefits of different disposal methods, and changes in technology.

2. Gramm-Leach-Bliley Act ("GLBA")

The Gramm-Leach-Bliley Act ("GLBA"), also known as the "Financial Services Modernization Act," was enacted in 1999. It applies to institutions that are <u>significantly engaged</u> in financial activities in the United States (also known as "domestic financial institutions"). These domestic financial institutions typically include banks, auto dealers, savings and loans, credit unions, insurance companies, brokerages, and securities firms. The GLBA sets forth two important rules that domestic financial institutions must adhere to: (1) the Privacy Rule and (2) the Safeguards Rule.

In accordance with the Privacy Rule, domestic financial institutions are required to provide an initial privacy notice to all <u>customers</u> when the customer relationship is established and annually thereafter. The privacy notice must be given to individual customers by mail or in-person delivery. Other reasonable ways to deliver the notice are also acceptable and depend on the type of business the institution is engaged in. For example, an online lender may post its notice on its website and require online customers to acknowledge receipt as a necessary part of a loan application.

The GLBA distinguishes "customers" from mere "consumers." A consumer is a person who obtains or has obtained a financial product or service from a financial institution that is to be used primarily for personal, family, or household purposes. A customer, on the other hand, is a consumer with a continuing relationship with a financial institution. Accordingly, it is the nature of the relationship that defines who is a customer and who is a consumer. Examples of customer relationships include (1) opening a credit card account with a financial institution, (2) leasing an automobile from an auto dealer, (3) using the services of a mortgage broker to secure financing, (4) obtaining the services of a tax preparer or investment adviser, and (5) getting a loan from a mortgage lender or payday lender.

Again, in accordance with the GLBA, customers (and not mere consumers) must be provided a copy of the financial institution's privacy notice when the customer relationship begins (and annually thereafter).

The privacy notice must be a clear, conspicuous, and accurate statement of the company's privacy practices. It should also include what information the company collects about its consumers and customers, with whom it shares the information, and how it protects or safeguards the information.

The GLBA also requires domestic financial institutions to provide opt-out notice prior to sharing non-public personal information ("NPI") with unaffiliated third parties. NPI includes any personally identifiable financial information that a financial institution collects about an individual in connection with providing a financial product or service, unless that information is otherwise publicly available. Examples of NPI include a customer's name, address, income, Social Security number, and other account-related information, such as account numbers, payment history, loan or deposit balances, and credit or debit card purchases. In accordance with the Privacy Rule, the mechanism provided for opting out must be reasonable, and the financial institution must provide a reasonable amount of time for the customer to opt out (for example, 30 days).

As you should recall, opt-out notice occurs when a data processor notifies a data subject about planned processing of his personal information and provides the data subject the opportunity to opt out of the processing. For example, if a bank informs a customer that his data will be shared with an unaffiliated marketing company unless he notifies the bank within thirty days, the bank is providing the customer with opt-out notice.

For your exam, it is important to remember that opt-out notice is only required under the GLBA when sharing personal information with non-affiliated third parties. No notice is required if the financial institution is sharing personal information with an affiliate. An affiliate is a company that controls, is controlled by, or is under common control with the financial institution.

In accordance with the Safeguards Rule, domestic financial institutions must develop a written information security plan protecting customer information. The plan must be appropriate to the company's size and complexity, the nature and scope of its activities, and the sensitivity of the customer information it handles. As part of its plan, each company must:

- Designate one or more employees to coordinate its information security program;

- Identify and assess the risks to customer information in each relevant area of the company's operation, and evaluate the effectiveness of the current safeguards for controlling these risks;
- Design and implement a safeguards program, and regularly monitor and test it;
- Select service providers that can maintain appropriate safeguards, make sure your contract requires them to maintain safeguards, and oversee their handling of customer information; and
- Evaluate and adjust the program in light of relevant circumstances, including changes in the firm's business or operations, or the results of security testing and monitoring.

Other important provisions of the GLBA also impact how financial institutions conduct business. For example, domestic financial institutions are prohibited from disclosing their customers' account numbers to non-affiliated companies when it comes to telemarketing, direct mail marketing or marketing through email.

Another provision of the GLBA prohibits "pretexting" – the practice of obtaining customer information from financial institutions under false pretenses. The FTC has recently brought several cases against information brokers who allegedly engaged in pretexting.

The agency responsible for enforcing the GLBA depends upon the type of financial institution. For example, banks, credit unions, and other affiliated financial institutions are regulated by multiple federal agencies, including the Office of the Comptroller of the Currency, the Federal Reserve Board, the Federal

Deposit Insurance Corporation ("FDIC"), Office of Thrift Supervision, and the National Credit Union Administration. The Securities and Exchange Commission ("SEC") is the designated agency for brokers, dealers, investment advisers, and investment companies. Lastly, the Federal Trade Commission ("FTC") is responsible for regulating all other financial institutions not otherwise subject to the enforcement authority of another regulator.

3. Dodd-Frank Wall Street Reform and Consumer Protection Act ("Dodd-Frank Act")

The Dodd-Frank Act was signed into law by President Obama in 2010. The Act's stated purposes are to (1) promote the financial stability of the United States by improving accountability and transparency within the financial system, (2) end "too big to fail," (3) protect the American taxpayer by ending bailouts, and (4) protect American consumers from abusive financial services practices.

The Dodd-Frank Act established the Consumer Financial Protection Bureau ("CFPB"), an independent agency of the United States government responsible for consumer protection in the financial sector. The CFPB was designed to consolidate employees and responsibilities from a number of other federal regulatory bodies, including the Federal Reserve, the Federal Trade Commission ("FTC"), the Federal Deposit Insurance Corporation ("FDIC"), the National Credit Union Administration and even the Department of Housing and Urban Development ("HUD").

The jurisdiction of the CFPB includes banks, credit unions, securities firms, payday lenders, mortgage-servicing operations, foreclosure relief services, debt collectors and other financial companies operating in the United States.

The mission of the CFPB is to protect consumers by carrying out federal consumer financial laws. To that end, the CFPB writes rules, supervises companies, and enforces federal consumer financial protection laws. In addition, the CFPB restricts unfair, deceptive, or abusive acts or practices, takes consumer complaints, promotes financial education, monitors financial markets for new risks to consumers, and enforces laws that outlaw discrimination and other unfair treatment in consumer finance.

4. Bank Secrecy Act ("BSA")

The Bank Secrecy Act ("BSA") of 1970, also known as the Currency and Foreign Transactions Reporting Act, requires financial institutions in the United States to assist government agencies in detecting and preventing money laundering.

Specifically, the act requires financial institutions to keep records of cash purchases of negotiable instruments, file reports of cash purchases of these negotiable instruments of more than $10,000 (daily aggregate amount), and report suspicious activity that might signify money laundering, tax evasion, or other criminal activities. Currency Transaction Reports ("CTRs") and Suspicious Activity Reports ("SARs") are the primary means used by banks to satisfy the requirements of the BSA.

Section 314(b) of the USA PATRIOT Act encourages financial institutions and financial institution associations (for example, bank trade groups and associations) to share information on individuals, entities, organizations, and countries (1) suspected of engaging in possible terrorist activity or (2) money laundering. Therefore, the BSA and USA PATRIOT Act provide financial institutions with broad discretion in detecting and preventing money laundering.

Violations of the BSA may result in both civil and criminal penalties. With respect to civil penalties, negligent violations of any regulation of the BSA may result in a fine of up to $500 per occurrence. Willful violations of any reporting requirement may result in a civil penalty of between $25,000 and $100,000 for financial institutions. The USA PATRIOT Act increased the maximum civil penalties for certain violations to between $100,000 and $1,000,000. Criminal penalties of up to $10,000 and 5 years imprisonment are also authorized.

D. Privacy Laws Regulating the Education Industry

The education industry generates a large amount of personal information relating to students. The primary federal law regulating the processing education records is the Family Educational Rights and Privacy Act ("FERPA"), as discussed more fully below.

1. Family Educational Rights and Privacy Act ("FERPA")

The Family Educational Rights and Privacy Act ("FERPA") was enacted in 1974 and subsequently updated by the Protection of Pupil Rights Amendment ("PPRA") in 1978. The primary purpose of FERPA is to protect the privacy of student education records. The law applies to all schools that receive funds under an applicable program of the U.S. Department of Education.

FERPA gives parents several rights with respect to their children's education records. These rights transfer to the student when he or she reaches the age of 18 or attends a school beyond the high school level. Students to whom the rights have transferred are called "eligible students."

First, parents or eligible students have the right to inspect and review the student's education records maintained by the school. Schools are not required to provide copies of records unless, for reasons such as great distance, it is impossible for parents or eligible students to review the records in person. Schools may charge a fee for copies.

Second, parents or eligible students have the right to request that a school correct records which they believe to be inaccurate or misleading. If the school decides not to amend the record, the parent or eligible student then has the right to a formal hearing. After the hearing, if the school still decides not to amend the record, the parent or eligible student has the right to place a statement with the record setting forth his or her view about the contested information.

For the purposes of FERPA, education records include all records that contain information directly related to a student and which are maintained by an educational agency, including report cards, transcripts, disciplinary records, contact and family information, and class schedules.

Generally, schools must have written permission from the parent or eligible student in order to release any information from a student's education record. However, FERPA allows schools to disclose those records, without consent, to the following parties or under the following conditions:

- School officials with legitimate educational interest;
- Other schools to which a student is transferring;
- Specified officials for audit or evaluation purposes;
- Appropriate parties in connection with financial aid to a student;
- Organizations conducting certain studies for or on behalf of the school;
- Accrediting organizations;
- To comply with a judicial order or lawfully issued subpoena;
- Appropriate officials in cases of health and safety emergencies; and
- State and local authorities, within a juvenile justice system, pursuant to specific State law.

Schools may also disclose, without consent, "directory" information, such as a student's name, address, telephone number, date and place of birth, honors and awards, and dates of attendance. However, schools must inform parents and eligible students about the planned disclosure of directory information and allow them a reasonable amount of time to opt out.

Schools must also notify parents and eligible students annually of their rights under FERPA. The actual means of notification (e.g., a special letter, inclusion in a PTA bulletin, student handbook, or newspaper article) is left to the discretion of each school.

The Protection of Pupil Rights Amendment ("PPRA") of 1978 amended FERPA in two ways. First, it requires that schools and contractors make instructional materials available for inspection by parents if those materials will be used in connection with a Department of Education funded survey, analysis, or evaluation in which their children participate.

Second, it requires that schools and contractors obtain written parental consent before minor students are required to participate in any Department of Education funded survey, analysis, or evaluation that reveals sensitive information, such as political affiliations, mental and psychological problems, sex behavior and attitudes, or parental income.

E. Privacy Laws Regulating the Marketing Industry

The Federal Trade Commission ("FTC") issued amendments to its Telemarketing Sales Rule ("TSR") in 2003, 2008, and 2010. Like the original TSR issued in 1995, the amended Rule is designed to supplement the Telemarketing and Consumer Fraud and Abuse Prevention Act of 1994. This legislation provides the FTC and state attorneys general a means to combat telemarketing fraud, while giving consumers added privacy protections and defenses against unscrupulous telemarketers.

1. Telemarketing Sales Rule ("TSR")

The FTC's Telemarketing Sales Rule ("TSR") puts consumers in charge of the number of telemarketing calls they receive at home. The TSR established the National Do Not Call Registry, which makes it easier and more efficient for consumers to reduce the number of unwanted telemarketing sales calls they receive. The FTC, the Federal Communications Commission ("FCC") and individual states began enforcing the National Do Not Call Registry on October 1, 2003.

The National Do Not Call Registry requires telemarketers to search the registry every 31 days and avoid calling any phone numbers that are on the registry. If an individual receives a telemarketing call after he has registered his telephone number and it has been in the registry for 31 days, he can file a complaint. A telemarketer who disregards the National Do Not Call Registry could be fined up to $16,000 for each call.

Placing your number on the National Do Not Call Registry will stop most telemarketing calls but not all. Calls from or on behalf of political organizations, charities, and telephone surveyors are still permitted.

Organizations with which you have an established business relationship ("EBR") can also call you for up to 18 months after your last purchase, payment or delivery — even if your number is on the National Do Not Call Registry. Furthermore, companies to which you have made an inquiry or submitted an application may call you for up to three months after your initial contact with them.

Even if you place your number on the national registry, you may still provide written permission for particular companies to call you. Alternately, if you have an established business relationship, you still can ask the company not to call you. The company must honor your request, regardless of any prior written permission.

And, if you don't put your number on the national registry, you still can prohibit individual telemarketers from calling, by asking each to put you on their company-specific internal do not call list. For record-keeping purposes, you should document the date you make the request and the person you spoke with.

One more important point: Although callers soliciting charitable contributions do not have to search the national registry, a for-profit telemarketer calling on behalf of a charitable organization must honor your request not to receive calls on behalf of that charity. Therefore, the TSR does provide a mechanism for preventing some calls from charitable organizations.

The TSR also prohibits deceptive and abusive telemarketing acts and practices and sets forth standards of conduct for telemarketing calls. Specifically, calling times are restricted to the hours between 8 AM and 9 PM. Telemarketers must also promptly tell you the identity of the seller or charitable organization and that the call is a sales call or a charitable solicitation. In addition, telemarketers must disclose all material information about the goods or services they are offering and the terms of the sale. They are also prohibited from lying about any terms of their offer.

Additionally, before submitting your billing information for payment, telemarketers must get your express informed consent to be charged — and to charge to a specific account. Telemarketers are also required to connect their call to a sales representative within two seconds of the consumer's greeting. Telemarketers must also transmit their telephone number and if possible, their name, to your caller ID service. This protects your privacy, increases accountability on the telemarketer's part, and helps in law enforcement efforts. Finally, most businesses need your express written permission before they can call you with prerecorded telemarketing messages, or "robocalls."

2. Telephone Consumer Protection Act ("TCPA")

The Telephone Consumer Protection Act ("TCPA") was enacted in 1991. The Federal Communications Commission ("FCC") is responsible for issuing rules and regulations implementing the TCPA. Among other things, the TCPA allows individuals to file lawsuits and collect damages for receiving unsolicited telemarketing calls, faxes, pre-recorded calls or autodialed calls.

Effective October 16, 2013, anyone engaged in telemarketing needs prior express written consent to place artificial or prerecorded telemarketing calls to a residential phone line or wireless number, or to send text messages or place calls to a wireless number using an automatic telephone dialing system. The TCPA includes a private right-of-action provision allowing private claims for statutory damages of up to $500 per call or actual damages for any violations (or up to three times the statutory or actual damages for willful or knowing violations).

The TCPA and associated FCC rules generally prohibit most unsolicited fax advertisements. In addition, the Junk Fax Prevention Act ("JFPA"), passed by Congress in 2005, directs the FCC to amend its rules adopted pursuant to the TCPA regarding fax advertising. The FCC's rules: (1) codify an established business relationship ("EBR") exemption to the prohibition on sending unsolicited fax advertisements; (2) define EBR for unsolicited fax advertisements; (3) require the sender of fax advertisements to provide specified notice and contact information on the fax that allows recipients to "opt-out" of any future faxes from the sender; and (4) specify the circumstances under which a request to "opt-out" complies with the Act.

The JFPA also makes it illegal to send junk faxes into the United States from outside the country. Under the JFPA, the sender of an unsolicited advertisement sent to a person's fax machine is still liable for a minimum of $500 per page, and damages may also be trebled at the court's discretion upon a finding that the violation was willful or knowing. The statute is one of strict liability; even if a person sends an unsolicited advertisement by fax accidently, a minimum liability of $500 per page attaches. The only potential defense for the sender is if the transmission was protected by the existing business relationship ("EBR") exception, which is similar to the EBR exception contained in the Telemarketing Sales Rule ("TSR") previously discussed.

3. Controlling the Assault of Non-Solicited Pornography And Marketing ("CAN-SPAM") Act

The Controlling the Assault of Non-Solicited Pornography And Marketing ("CAN-SPAM") Act was enacted in 2003 to address the alarming increase in unsolicited commercial messages. The law sets forth rules for sending commercial messages, gives recipients the right to have you stop emailing them, and spells out tough penalties for violations.

Despite its name, the CAN-SPAM Act applies to more than just bulk email. It covers all electronic commercial messages, which the law defines as "any electronic mail message the primary purpose of which is the commercial advertisement or promotion of a commercial product or service," including email that promotes content on commercial websites. The law makes no exception for business-to-business email. All email – for example, a message to former customers announcing a new product line – must comply with the law.

The CAN-SPAM Act has seven main requirements:

- Don't use false or misleading header information in emails. Your "From," "To," "Reply-To," and routing information – including the originating domain name and email address – must be accurate and identify the person or business who initiated the message.

- Don't use deceptive subject lines. The subject line must accurately reflect the content of the message.
- Identify the message as an ad. The law gives you a lot of leeway in how to do this, but you must disclose clearly and conspicuously that your message is an advertisement.
- Tell recipients where you're located. Your message must include your valid physical postal address. This can be your current street address, a post office box you've registered with the U.S. Postal Service, or a private mailbox you've registered with a commercial mail-receiving agency established under Postal Service regulations.
- Tell recipients how to opt out of receiving future email from you. Your message must include a clear and conspicuous explanation of how the recipient can opt out of getting email from you in the future.
- Honor opt-out requests promptly. Any opt-out mechanism you offer must be able to process opt-out requests for at least 30 days after you send your message. You must honor a recipient's opt-out request within 10 business days. You can't charge a fee, require the recipient to give you any personally identifying information beyond an email address, or make the recipient take any step other than sending a reply email or visiting a single page on an Internet website as a condition for honoring an opt-out request.
- Monitor what others are doing on your behalf. The law makes clear that even if you hire another company to handle your email marketing, you can't contract away your legal responsibility to comply with the law. Both the

company whose product is promoted in the message and the company that actually sends the message may be held legally responsible.

Each email in violation of the CAN-SPAM Act is subject to a penalty of up to $16,000.

4. Cable Communications Policy Act ("CCPA")

The Cable Communications Policy Act was enacted in 1984 to promote competition and deregulate the cable industry. The statute requires cable operators to provide notice to subscribers regarding the nature of personal information being collected and the nature of the cable operator's use of the personal information.

In addition, the CCPA requires prior written or electronic consent before a cable operator may collect personal information. The CCPA also generally prohibits disclosure of personally identifiable information and requires a cable operator to take steps to prevent unauthorized access to personal information already collected.

Some exceptions to the collection and disclosure prohibitions exist. First, the CCPA permits collection of personal information if "necessary to render a cable service" or "detect unauthorized reception of cable communications." Second, the CCPA permits disclosure if the consumer failed to opt-out after the cable operator provided the opportunity opt-out, or if the disclosure does not reveal the extent of use or transactions made by the subscribers.

Cable operators must also provide the subscriber access to the personal information collected by the cable operator. Information that is no longer necessary for the purpose for which it was collected must also be destroyed.

In addition to any other remedies the consumer might have available, the CCPA provides for civil remedies that include: (1) reasonable attorney's fees; (2) damages not less than $100 per day or $1,000 per violation, whichever is greater; and (3) punitive damages.

5. Video Privacy Protection Act ("VPAA")

The Video Privacy Protection Act ("VPPA") was enacted in 1988 to prevent the wrongful disclosure of video tape rental or sale records of similar audio visual materials, such as video games and DVDs. The VPAA generally prohibits providers from knowingly disclosing the personal information of a consumer, including a consumer's video viewing history, to a third party unless the consumer consents specifically and in writing.

The VPAA also contains a requirement that video stores destroy rental records no longer than one year after an account is terminated.

The VPPA provides for a private right of action and permits a court to award statutory damages of at least $2,500 per violation and attorney's fees. The VPPA does not preempt state law. In other words, states are free to enact broader protections for video records.

F. Privacy Laws Regulating the Internet

Many of the privacy laws already discussed in this guide indirectly regulate activities performed on the

Internet. For example, the CAN-SPAM Act regulates the distribution of unsolicited commercial messages, including emails. Similarly, the Video Privacy Protection Act extends to purely Internet-based services, such as Netflix and Hulu.

Two important laws apply directly and solely to the Internet: (1) the Children's Online Privacy Protection Act ("COPPA"); and (2) the California Online Privacy Protection Act Online ("CalOPPA").

1. Children's Online Privacy Protection Act ("COPPA")

The Children's Online Privacy Protection Act ("COPPA") was enacted in 1998 to curtail the collection of personal information from children. COPPA required the Federal Trade Commission ("FTC") to issue and enforce regulations concerning children's online privacy. The FTC's original COPPA Rule became effective on April 21, 2000.

The primary goal of COPPA is to place parents in control over what information is collected from their young children online. The Rule was designed to protect children under the age of 13 while embracing the dynamic and interactive nature of the Internet.

The Rule applies to (1) operators of commercial websites and online services (including mobile applications) directed to children under the age of 13 that collect, use, or disclose personal information from children, and (2) operators of general audience websites or online services with actual knowledge that they are collecting, using, or disclosing personal information from children under the age of 13.

The Rule also applies to websites or online services that have actual knowledge that they are collecting personal information directly from users of another third-party website or online service directed to children.

Operators covered by the Rule must:

- Post a clear and comprehensive online privacy policy describing their information practices for personal information collected online from children;

- Provide direct notice to parents and obtain verifiable parental consent, with limited exceptions, before collecting personal information online from children;

- Give parents the choice of consenting to the operator's collection and internal use of a child's information, but prohibiting the operator from disclosing that information to third parties (unless disclosure is integral to the site or service, in which case, this must be made clear to parents);

- Provide parents access to their child's personal information to review and/or have the information deleted;

- Give parents the opportunity to prevent further use or online collection of a child's personal information;

- Maintain the confidentiality, security, and integrity of information they collect from children, including by taking reasonable steps to release such information only to parties capable of maintaining its confidentiality and security; and

- Retain personal information collected online from a child for only as long as is necessary to fulfill the purpose for which it was collected and delete the information using reasonable measures to protect against its unauthorized access or use.

The FTC's amended COPPA rule went into effect on July 1, 2013. It added four new categories of information to the definition of personal information: (1) geolocation information, (2) photos or videos containing a child's image or audio files with a child's voice; (3) screen or user name; and (4) persistent identifiers that can be used to recognize a user over time and across different websites or online services.

Violations of COPPA may result in civil liability of up to $16,000 per violation after considering numerous factors, including the egregiousness of the violation, whether the operator has previously violated the Rule, the number of children involved, the amount and type of personal information collected, how the information was used, whether it was shared with third parties, and the size of the company.

2. California Online Privacy Protection Act Online ("CalOPPA")

Enacted in 2003, the California Online Privacy Protection Act Online ("CalOPPA") requires operators of commercial websites that collect personally identifiable information from California residents to conspicuously post and comply with a privacy policy that meets certain requirements.

In accordance with CalOPPA, the operator of a website must post a distinctive and easily found link to the website's privacy policy. The privacy policy must detail the kinds of information gathered by the website, how the information may be shared with other parties, and, if such a process exists, describe the process that the user can utilize to review and make changes to their stored information. It also must include the policy's effective date and a description of any changes since the effective date.

Although the Act only technically applies to the collection of personal information of California residents, many website operators are forced to comply by virtue of serving the Californian market. Therefore, this state law has broad applicability.

Those who fail to comply with CalOPPA are in violation of the statute if they do not post a compliant privacy policy within 30 days of being notified of their noncompliance. While CalOPPA does not provide for a private right of action, the California attorney general can bring enforcement actions under the law. In addition, violations of CalOPPA may result in civil penalties of up to $2,500 per violation.

Chapter 7: Government Access to Personal Information

This chapter addresses the major privacy laws that regulate the disclosure of personal information during a government investigation or in connection with a court proceeding, such as an administrative, civil, or criminal trial. You should expect anywhere from 6 to 10 questions on your examination directed to subject matter from this chapter.

A. Glossary Terms

Although the subject matter discussed in this chapter is not heavily tested, the privacy implications of governmental investigations and court orders are part of the toolkit that a certified information privacy profession should possess. Therefore, you should review the definitions provided in the glossary for the terms listed below. The glossary is located at:

http://www.cippexam.com/glossary

Glossary Terms: Article 29 Working Party, Digital Fingerprinting, Electronic Discovery, Electronic Communications Privacy Act of 1986, Electronic Surveillance, Freedom of Information Act, National Security Letter, Protective Order, Qualified Protective Order, Redaction, Sedona Conference, Stored Communications Act, USA-PATRIOT Act.

B. Disclosures Required by Law

Most privacy laws that restrict the disclosure of personal information have an exception for disclosures required by law. For example, in accordance with

HIPAA, a covered entity may use or disclose protected health information without the written authorization of the individual "to the extent that such use or disclosure is required by law and the use or disclosure complies with and is limited to the relevant requirements of such law." In addition, a covered entity may disclose protected health information in the course of any judicial or administrative proceeding when in response to (1) an order of the court or administrative tribunal, or (2) a subpoena, discovery request, or other lawful form of process.

1. Discovery Requests and Subpoenas

Once a case has been filed with an appropriate federal or state court, the parties to the court action (called "litigants") are generally free to request discovery from each other and other third parties for the purposes of helping prove their case. Discovery is the compulsory disclosure of relevant documents or testimony requested by a party to a court action.

Typically, a discovery request from one party is "served" on the party whom possess the requested information. Service is the procedure by which a party to a lawsuit gives an appropriate notice to another person. Generally, service is effectuated by hand delivering a copy of the discovery request to the person who retains or controls the requested information.

A discovery request typically requires a person to produce documents or testify at a deposition. When serving a discovery request on a third party who is not part of the court action, a subpoena is generally required. A subpoena is a formal order from a court or other governmental agency compelling the third party to comply with a discovery request.

Generally, a party may obtain discovery regarding any non-privileged matter that is relevant to any party's claim or defense—including the existence, description, nature, custody, condition, and location of any documents or other tangible things and the identity and location of persons who know of any discoverable matter.

A party who does not comply with a subpoena or discovery request may be sanctioned by the court or governmental agency issuing the subpoena or request. Sanctions may include monetary fines and the opposing party's reasonable expenses, including attorney's fees.

A party or any person from whom discovery is sought may move for a <u>protective order</u> in the court where the action is pending if the person believes that compliance with the discovery request would cause a clearly defined and serious injury to that person. For example, Rule 26 of the Federal Rules of Civil Procedure provides that "any person from whom discovery is sought may move for a protective order in the court where the action is pending … to protect a party or person from annoyance, embarrassment, oppression, or undue burden or expense."

When evaluating requests for protective orders, courts have considered various factors, including the confidentiality interests at issue, the need to protect public health and safety, the fairness and efficiency of entering a protective order, and the importance of the litigation to the public.

2. Public Access to Court Records

In the United States, the general rule is that the public has access to all court filings and records. Public access to court records ensures a degree of transparency in the judicial process. If a document contains sensitive information, such as a trade secret or confidential financial data, a party may ask the court to redact certain portions of the document (or alternatively seek a protective order). Redaction is the process of removing or obscuring sensitive portions of a document. For example, all but the last four digits of an individual's social security number should be redacted from a document before filing it with a federal court.

Alternatively, if an entire document contains sensitive information, a court may require that the document be filed "under seal." When filed under seal, the entire document is inaccessible to the public. The court may later unseal the filing or order the person who made the filing to file a redacted version for the public record. Because sealing a document is counter to the presumption of public access to judicial records, courts generally require a compelling reason before authorizing documents to be filed under seal.

3. Electronic Discovery

A large portion of discoverable information today is electronic. Electronic discovery refers to the production of electronically stored information (commonly called "ESI") during the course of a governmental investigation or court proceeding. In accordance with state and federal discovery rules, electronically stored information is generally discoverable so long as it is relevant to an issue in the case.

Electronically stored information includes email, web pages, word processing files and spreadsheets, audio and video files, images, computer databases, metadata, and virtually anything else that is stored on an electronic storage medium – including, but not limited to, servers, desktops, laptops, smartphones, hard drives, flash drives, PDAs and MP3 players. In accordance with document preservation rules, organizations are required to properly preserve electronically stored information when litigation is "reasonably foreseeable."

In 2002, the Sedona Conference Working Group on Electronic Document Retention and Production, a group of attorneys and others experienced in electronic discovery matters, met to address the production of electronic information in discovery. The group was concerned about whether rules and concepts developed largely for paper discovery would be adequate for electronic discovery. After debate, a set of core principles emerged for addressing the production of electronic information. These principles became known as The Sedona Principles, and today represent the best practices for electronic discovery.

C. Federal Laws Regulating Government Investigations

The Fourth Amendment to the United States Constitution originally enforced the notion that "each man's home is his castle," secure from unreasonable searches and seizures of property by the government. The Fourth Amendment protects against arbitrary arrests and is the basis of law regarding search warrants, stop-and-frisk tactics, safety inspections, wiretaps, and other forms of surveillance. The Supreme Court has stated that the fundamental purpose of the Fourth Amendment is to guarantee "the privacy, dignity and security of persons against certain arbitrary and invasive acts by officers of the Government."

In addition to the Fourth Amendment, several important federal laws have been enacted that proscribe or set limits to the conduct of the United States government. These laws include (1) the Federal Wiretap Act; (2) the Electronic Communications Privacy Act ("ECPA"); (3) the Communications Assistance for Law Enforcement Act ("CALEA"); (4) the Right to Financial Privacy Act; and (5) the Privacy Protection Act ("PPA"). Each of these laws is discussed below in turn.

1. Federal Wiretap Act

The Federal Wiretap Act was enacted in 1968 as Title III of the Omnibus Crime Control and Safe Streets Act. The Federal Wiretap Act originally regulated only wire (that is, telephone) and oral communications, but was later extended to additionally include all electronic communications.

The Federal Wiretap Act broadly prohibits the intentional interception, use, or disclosure of all wired and electronic communications unless a statutory exception applies. In general, this prohibition bars all third parties (including the government) from wiretapping telephones and installing electronic surveillance equipment (known as "sniffers") from reading Internet traffic. It also bars all third parties from disclosing or using the <u>actual contents</u> of the intercepted communication. The Act, however, does not prohibit the disclosure or use of transactional information about the communication, such as the time, date, and length of the communication, as well as the participants to the communication.

Before a wiretapping order is issued, law enforcement personnel must submit a detailed application to a federal judge. The judge will issue a wiretap order only if the application reveals probable cause to believe that the interception will reveal evidence of a felony. When authorized, a wiretap order permits law enforcement to intercept communications for up to thirty days.

Two notable exceptions to the Federal Wiretap Act's broad prohibition against interception of communications exist. First, under federal law, if one party to the communication consents to the interception, it is permitted. Under most state laws, however, consent of both parties is required. Second, operators are authorized to intercept and monitor communications placed over their facilities in order to combat fraud and theft of service. Unless one of these two exceptions exist, a wiretap order is required before intercepting communications.

2. Electronic Communications Privacy Act ("ECPA")

The Electronic Communications Privacy Act ("ECPA") was enacted in 1986 to update the Federal Wiretap Act. ECPA protects wire, oral, and electronic communications while those communications are being made, are in transit, and when they are stored on computers. Therefore, ECPA applies to email, telephone conversations, and data stored electronically.

ECPA has three titles. Title I expands the Federal Wiretap Act to prohibit the intentional, actual or attempted interception, use, disclosure, or procurement of the contents of any wire, oral, or electronic communication. Title I also prohibits the use of illegally obtained communications as evidence in a court or other governmental proceeding.

Title II of the ECPA, which is called the Stored Communications Act ("SCA"), protects the privacy of the contents of files stored by service providers and of records held by service providers relating to a subscriber, such as the subscriber's name, billing records, or IP address.

Title III of the ECPA, which addresses pen register and trap and trace devices, requires government entities to obtain a court order authorizing the installation and use of a pen register (a device that captures the dialed numbers of outgoing calls) and/or a trap and trace device (a device that captures the numbers of incoming calls).

Pen registers and trap and trace devices capture only transactional information, such as telephone numbers and the duration of the communication. They do not record the actual contents of the communication. Therefore, pen registers and trap and trace devices do not generally violate the Federal Wiretap Act.

In accordance with ECPA, a court may issue a pen register or trap and trace order once an applicant certifies that the information likely to be obtained is relevant to an ongoing criminal investigation being conducted by the applicant's agency. Therefore, the threshold for obtaining a pen register or trap and trace order is substantially lower than that for a wiretap, which requires probable cause that a felony is being committed.

3. Communications Assistance for Law Enforcement Act ("CALEA")

In response to concerns that emerging technologies, such as digital and wireless communications, were making it increasingly difficult for law enforcement agencies to execute authorized surveillance, Congress enacted the Communications Assistance for Law Enforcement Act ("CALEA") in 1994.

CALEA requires telecommunications carriers to ensure that their equipment, facilities, and services enable enforcement officials to conduct electronic surveillance pursuant to a court order or other lawful authorization. CALEA was intended to preserve the ability of law enforcement agencies to conduct electronic surveillance by requiring that telecommunications carriers and manufacturers of telecommunications equipment modify and design their equipment, facilities, and services to ensure that they have the necessary surveillance capabilities.

In 2006, the Federal Communications Commission ("FCC") issued a Second Report and Order that required facilities-based broadband Internet access providers and providers of interconnected Voice over Internet Protocol ("VoIP") service to comply with CALEA obligations.

A telecommunications carrier may comply with CALEA in several different ways. First, the carrier may develop its own compliance solution with surveillance capability for its unique network. Second, the carrier may purchase a compliance solution with surveillance capability from vendors, including the manufacturers of the equipment it is using to provide service. Finally, the carrier may purchase a compliance solution with surveillance capability from a trusted third party.

4. Right to Financial Privacy Act

The Right to Financial Privacy Act was enacted in 1978 to protect the confidentiality of financial records. The Act governs disclosures to the federal government, its officers, agents, agencies, and departments. It does not govern private businesses or state or local government.

The Act prohibits financial institutions from disclosing a customer's financial records to the federal government except in limited circumstances, including pursuant to (1) the customer's authorization, (2) an administrative subpoena or summons, (3) a search warrant, and (4) a judicial subpoena or formal written request in connection with a legitimate law enforcement inquiry.

5. Privacy Protection Act ("PPA")

The Privacy Protection Act ("PPA") was enacted in 1980 to protect journalists and newsrooms from searches by government officials. The Act was passed in response to a 1978 Supreme Court decision holding that a search of the offices of the Stanford Daily, a student newspaper published at Stanford University, was constitutional because a search warrant had been duly issued for the search. The Act generally prevents the government from seizing a journalist's materials during an investigation.

Specifically, the Act prohibits "a government officer or employee, in connection with the investigation or prosecution of a criminal offense, to search for or seize any work product materials possessed by a person reasonably believed to have a purpose to disseminate to the public a newspaper, book, broadcast, or other similar form of public communication."

The Act protects both work product and documentary materials. To obtain a journalist's materials, the government is first generally required to obtain a subpoena from a court. The subpoena will provide the journalist with a definite amount of time to respond and the opportunity to challenge the validity of the subpoena.

Search or seizure without a subpoena is only permitted if (1) immediate seizure of the material is necessary to prevent death or serious bodily injury, or (2) there is probable cause to believe that the person possessing the materials has committed or is committing a criminal offense to which the materials relate.

D. Privacy and National Security

In the wake of the terrorist acts of September 11, 2001, national security has become an important and sensitive topic. Privacy laws seek to balance the government's legitimate need for access to information relevant to our country's national security interests with an individual's right to privacy. The

Foreign Intelligence Surveillance Act ("FISA") and USA PATRIOT Act are two important laws that permit government access to information under circumstances that may implicate national security. Each of these laws in discussed below in turn.

1. Foreign Intelligence Surveillance Act ("FISA")

The Foreign Intelligence Surveillance Act ("FISA") was enacted in 1978 in response to revelations regarding the government's past abuses of electronic surveillance for national security purposes. The Act was also designed to clarify the somewhat uncertain state of the law on surveillance for national security purposes.

While FISA today provides a statutory framework for a wide array of surveillance techniques, the original 1978 Act dealt solely with electronic surveillance. The act has been amended repeatedly in the intervening years in an effort to address changing circumstances. Then, as now, the law attempts to strike a balance between national security interests and civil liberties.

FISA establishes two special courts: (1) the U.S. Foreign Intelligence Surveillance Court ("FISC") and (2) the U.S. Foreign Intelligence Surveillance Court of Review ("Court of Review"), both of which are comprised of federal judges. These courts receive and review applications for court orders authorizing electronic surveillance, physical searches, installation and use of pen registers and trap and trace devices, and production of tangible things.

In accordance with FISA, surveillance is generally conducted under an FISC order, unless the surveillance fits within one of three statutory exceptions. The first of these exceptions is the electronic surveillance of foreign powers for up to one year without a court order upon Attorney General certification. A foreign power is defined as (1) a foreign government or any component thereof, whether or not recognized by the United States; (2) a faction of a foreign nation or nations, not substantially composed of United States persons; or (3) an entity that is openly acknowledged by a foreign government or governments to be directed and controlled by such foreign government or governments.

The second exception is the emergency electronic surveillance upon Attorney General certification for up to 72 hours while an FISC order is being sought.

Finally, the third exception is the electronic surveillance for 15 calendar days after a congressional declaration of war.

If an exception does not apply, a FISC order is required before surveillance may commence. A federal officer may submit an application for a FISC order in writing on oath or affirmation to an FISC judge. The application will be approved if there is probable cause to believe that (A) the target of the electronic surveillance is a foreign power or an agent of a foreign power; and (B) each of the facilities or places at which the electronic surveillance is directed is being used, or is about to be used, by a foreign power or an agent of a foreign power. Denials of applications by the FISC may be appealed to the Court of Review.

FISA also contains "minimization requirements" that mandate certain procedures to minimize the collection, retention, and dissemination of information about United States persons. Before issuing a FISC order, the court must find that the proposed surveillance satisfies the minimization requirements.

Persons intentionally engaging in electronic surveillance not authorized by the statute under color of law (that is, with the appearance of legal power) may face criminal penalties. Criminal penalties also exist for those who disclose information known to have been obtained through unauthorized surveillance. Civil liability also exists for noncompliance with FISA.

2. USA PATRIOT Act

On October 26, 2001, President George W. Bush signed the Uniting and Strengthening America by Providing Appropriate Tools Required to Intercept and Obstruct Terrorism Act (or the USA PATRIOT Act). Among its provisions are several which impacted or amended the Foreign Intelligence Surveillance Act ("FISA"). The USA PATRIOT Act also expanded the authority of the government to issue national security letters ("NSLs"), which are administrative subpoenas issued by the Federal Bureau of Investigation ("FBI") in authorized national security investigations.

Today, there are five different federal statutes authorizing federal officials (typically the FBI) to request information by issuing NSLs. The statutes apply to communications providers, financial institutions, and credit bureaus. The requested information typically consists of customer business records, including subscriber and transactional information related to Internet and telephone usage, credit reports, and financial records.

Under these statutes, national security letters may be issued by officials at FBI headquarters or by heads of FBI field offices without prior approval from a judge. It is important to note, however, that national security letters cannot be used to obtain the contents of a communication. NSLs are limited to solely transactional or record information, such as bank statements.

A person receiving a national security letter may seek judicial review of the letter by petitioning a federal court for an order modifying or setting aside the request. The federal court may modify or quash the NSL request if compliance would be unreasonable, oppressive, or otherwise unlawful.

Generally, an NSL must be relevant to an investigation to protect against international terrorism or foreign spying. The information being sought does not, however, need to pertain to a foreign power or its agents, rendering the potential scope of an NSL quite broad. For example, an NSL may compel a communications provider, such as AT&T or Comcast, to turn over its billing records related to phone numbers called by a suspected terrorist.

In addition, entities receiving an NSL may be prohibited from disclosing the fact that that they received an NSL if the investigative agency has certified that disclosure may endanger any individual or the national security of the United States, interfere with diplomatic relations, or interfere with a criminal or intelligence investigation. This non-disclosure requirement is commonly referred to as a "gag order" and may be challenged by the recipient of the NSL in federal court.

Chapter 8: Privacy in the Workplace

This chapter addresses the major privacy laws that regulate the workplace in the United States. You should expect anywhere from 7 to 11 questions on your examination directed to workplace privacy issues.

A. Glossary Terms

Your exam will contain numerous questions testing material from this chapter. Therefore, it is important that you read the definitions provided in the glossary for the terms listed below. The glossary is located at:

http://www.cippexam.com/glossary

Glossary Terms: Americans with Disabilities Act, Antidiscrimination Laws, Background Screening/Checks, California Investigative Consumer Reporting Agencies Act, Closed Circuit Television, Defamation, Employee Information, Employment at Will, Equal Employment Opportunity Commission, Location-Based Service, National Labor Relations Board, Publicity Given to Private Life, Random Testing, Reasonable Suspicion, Sarbanes-Oxley Act, Substance Testing, U.S. Department of Labor, Video Surveillance, Whistle-Blowing.

B. Overview of Workplace Privacy

As you may recall, the Fourth Amendment of the U.S. Constitution prohibits government agents from conducting unreasonable searches and seizures. However, because this prohibition requires state action and does not generally apply to conduct of private parties, it does not protect the privacy of a typical employee working at a private company. Some employer activities that may raise issues of workplace privacy include drug testing or screening, workplace and employee searches, surveillance by audio or video tape recordings, and monitoring of off-duty conduct.

In the United States, the relationship between an employer and an employee is generally defined by contract law. Typically, an employee will enter into an employment agreement with his employer that defines the scope of the employment. Other corporate documents, such as a company's employee handbook, may also create binding obligations for both the employer and the employee.

Sometimes, organizations representing a plurality of employees may enter into a collective bargaining agreement with the employer that defines the employment relationship for all covered individuals. These collective bargaining agreements may even specify certain privacy protections, such as limits to drug testing or screening. Collective bargaining agreements are generally used when a union is representing a large block of employees.

Finally, in the United States, an employer typically hires an employee under the employment-at-will doctrine, which provides that both the employee and the employer may terminate the employment relationship for any reason and at any time. This at-will status also applies by default when employees are hired without a written employment contract. Therefore, employers are free to terminate employees for any legitimate reason. The only exception is that employers may not terminate an employee based on discrimination or retaliation, which will be discussed more fully in Section D of this chapter.

C. Invasion of Privacy Torts

Torts are broadly defined as civil wrongs recognized by law as grounds for a lawsuit. Invasion of privacy is a term that describes a collection of torts that protect employees at their workplace from unreasonable conduct by their employers. Invasion of privacy includes (1) intrusion into seclusion, (2) public disclosure of private facts, and (3) portrayal in a false light.

Intrusion into seclusion occurs when an employer intentionally intrudes, physically or otherwise, upon the solitude or seclusion of another or his private affairs or concerns. This tort requires the intrusion to be highly offensive to a reasonable person. For example, conducting video surveillance in a locker room or bathroom would be highly offensive to a reasonable person and therefore may constitute an intrusion into the seclusion of an employee if done at the workplace.

Public disclosure of private facts occurs when an employer gives publicity to a matter concerning the private life of another if the matter publicized is of a kind that would be highly offensive to a reasonable person and is not of legitimate concern to the public. For example, if an employer issues a press release indicating that a specific employee has a serious, life threatening medical condition, this press release may constitute the public disclosure of private facts.

Portrayal in a false light occurs when an employer gives publicity to a matter concerning another that places the other before the public in a false light if the false light in which the other was placed would be highly offensive to a reasonable person, and if the actor had knowledge of or acted in reckless disregard as to the falsity of the publicized matter and the false light in which the other would be placed.

False light invasion of privacy claims are very similar to another tort called defamation. In fact, these two torts are often alleged together. Defamation is a written (called "libel") or oral (called "slander") publication of a false statement to a third party that tends to diminish the esteem, respect, goodwill or confidence of the employee to excite adverse, derogatory or unpleasant feelings or opinions against the employee.

While false light requires dissemination to the public at large, defamation may occur when the false statement is published to only a single third-party. Therefore, false light and defamation differ mainly in the size of the audience that receives the defamatory information. Terminated employees frequently file claims for defamation and/or false light over their employer's release of information surrounding their termination.

Although tort law in theory provides some degree of privacy protection to employees, it generally only applies to conduct that is highly offensive and egregious. In addition, the employer may invoke one of numerous defenses to the torts, including truth (that is, the statements are not in fact false) and employee consent (either express or implied). A qualified privilege also exists for information that is a matter of public concern, such as fair criticism or public safety.

D. Federal Laws Protecting Workplace Privacy

Numerous federal laws indirectly protect workplace privacy. For example, federal laws prohibiting discrimination prevent employers from making employment decisions based on areas that may be used to discriminate. Some of the more important antidiscrimination laws are discussed below.

Title VII of the Civil Rights Act of 1964 (Title VII) makes it illegal to discriminate against someone on the basis of race, color, religion, national origin, or sex. The law also makes it illegal to retaliate against a person because the person complained about discrimination, filed a charge of discrimination, or participated in an employment discrimination investigation or lawsuit. The law also requires that employers reasonably accommodate applicants' and employees' sincerely held religious practices, unless doing so would impose an undue hardship on the operation of the employer's business.

The Pregnancy Discrimination Act makes it illegal to discriminate against a woman because of pregnancy, childbirth, or a medical condition related to pregnancy or childbirth. The law also makes it illegal to retaliate against a person because the person complained about discrimination, filed a charge of discrimination, or participated in an employment discrimination investigation or lawsuit.

The Equal Pay Act of 1963 ("EPA") makes it illegal to pay different wages to men and women if they perform equal work in the same workplace. The law also makes it illegal to retaliate against a person because the person complained about discrimination, filed a charge of discrimination, or participated in an employment discrimination investigation or lawsuit.

The Age Discrimination in Employment Act of 1967 ("ADEA") protects people who are 40 or older from discrimination because of age. The law also makes it illegal to retaliate against a person because the person complained about discrimination, filed a charge of discrimination, or participated in an employment discrimination investigation or lawsuit.

Title I of the Americans with Disabilities Act of 1990 ("ADA") makes it illegal to discriminate against a qualified person with a disability in the private sector and in state and local governments. The law also makes it illegal to retaliate against a person because the person complained about discrimination, filed a charge of discrimination, or participated in an employment discrimination investigation or lawsuit. The law also requires that employers reasonably accommodate the known physical or mental limitations of an otherwise qualified individual with a disability who is an applicant or employee, unless doing so would impose an undue hardship on the operation of the employer's business.

As previously discussed in this guide, the Genetic Information Nondiscrimination Act of 2008 ("GINA") makes it illegal to discriminate against employees or applicants because of genetic information. Genetic information includes information about an individual's genetic tests and the genetic tests of an individual's family members, as well as information about any disease, disorder or condition of an individual's family members (that is, an individual's family medical history). The law also makes it illegal to retaliate against a person because the person complained about discrimination, filed a charge of discrimination, or participated in an employment discrimination investigation or lawsuit.

Each of these laws is enforced by the U.S. Equal Employment Opportunity Commission ("EEOC"). The EEOC is a federal agency responsible for enforcing federal laws that make it illegal to discriminate against a job applicant or an employee because of the person's race, color, religion, sex (including pregnancy), national origin, age (40 or older), disability or genetic information. It is also illegal to discriminate against a person because the person complained about discrimination, filed a charge of discrimination, or participated in an employment discrimination investigation or lawsuit.

Most employers with at least 15 employees are covered by EEOC laws (20 employees in age discrimination cases). Most labor unions and employment agencies are also covered. The laws apply to all types of work situations, including scenarios pertaining to hiring, firing, promotions, harassment, training, wages, and benefits.

The EEOC has the authority to investigate charges of discrimination against employers who are covered by the law. The EEOC's role in an investigation is to fairly and accurately assess the allegations in the charge and then make a finding. If the EEOC finds that discrimination has occurred, it will try to settle the charge. If the EEOC is not successful with a settlement, it has the authority to file a lawsuit to protect the rights of individuals and the interests of the public.

In addition to the EEOC, workplace privacy is protected by the Federal Trade Commission ("FTC"), National Labor Relations Board ("NLRB"), Department of Labor, and Consumer Financial Protection Bureau ("CFPB"). For example, The Occupational Safety and Health Act ("OSHA") of 1970 sets out safety requirements for workplaces and is governed and enforced by the Department of Labor. Similarly, the National Labor Relations Act, which protects workers who wish to form, join or support unions, or who are already represented by unions, is governed and enforced by the NLRB.

E. Privacy Issues Before, During, and After Employment

Numerous situations before, during, and after employment may violate an employee's legitimate privacy interests. These situations include (1) pre-employment screening and interviewing of an applicant (including background checks), (2) monitoring and investigating the conduct of an employee (for example, through routine drug testing and video surveillance), and (3) post termination activities, such as reference checks and recommendations.

1. Pre-Employment Practices

Under the laws enforced by Equal Employment Opportunity Commission ("EEOC"), it is illegal to discriminate against someone (whether an applicant or an employee) because of that person's race, color, religion, sex (including pregnancy), national origin, age (40 or older), disability or genetic information. It is also illegal to retaliate against a person because he or she complained about discrimination, filed a charge of discrimination, or participated in an employment discrimination investigation or lawsuit. The law forbids discrimination in every aspect of employment.

The laws enforced by EEOC also prohibit an employer or other covered entity from using neutral employment policies and practices that have a disproportionately negative effect on applicants or employees of a particular race, color, religion, sex (including pregnancy), or national origin, or on an individual with a disability or class of individuals with disabilities, if the polices or practices at issue are not job-related and necessary to the operation of the business.

The laws enforced by EEOC also prohibit an employer from using neutral employment policies and practices that have a disproportionately negative impact on applicants or employees age 40 or older if the policies or practices at issue are not based on a reasonable factor other than age.

It is illegal for an employer to publish a job advertisement that shows a preference for a candidate or discourages someone from applying for a job because of his or her race, color, religion, sex (including pregnancy), national origin, age (40 or older), disability or genetic information. For example, a help-wanted ad that seeks "females" or "recent college graduates" may discourage men and people over 40 from applying and may violate the law.

It is also illegal for an employer to recruit new employees in a way that discriminates against them because of their race, color, religion, sex (including pregnancy), national origin, age (40 or older), disability or genetic information. For example, an employer's reliance on word-of-mouth recruitment by its mostly Hispanic work force may violate the law if the result is that almost all new hires are Hispanic.

It is illegal for an employer to discriminate against a job applicant because of his or her race, color, religion, sex (including pregnancy), national origin, age (40 or older), disability or genetic information. For example, an employer may not refuse to give employment applications to people of a certain race.

An employer may also not base hiring decisions on stereotypes and assumptions about a person's race, color, religion, sex (including pregnancy), national origin, age (40 or older), disability or genetic information.

If an employer requires job applicants to take a test, the test must be necessary and related to the job, and the employer may not exclude people of a particular race, color, religion, sex (including pregnancy), national origin, or individuals with disabilities. In addition, the employer may not use a test that excludes applicants age 40 or older if the test is not based on a reasonable factor other than age. If a job applicant with a disability needs an accommodation (such as a sign language interpreter) to apply for a job, the employer is required to provide the accommodation, so long as the accommodation does not cause the employer significant difficulty or expense.

As a general rule, the information obtained and requested through the pre-employment screening process should be limited to those essential for determining if a person is qualified for the job; whereas, information regarding race, sex, national origin, age, and religion are irrelevant in such determinations. Although state and federal equal opportunity laws do not clearly forbid employers from making pre-employment inquiries that relate to, or disproportionately screen out members based on race, color, sex, national origin, religion, or age, such inquiries may be used as evidence of an employer's intent to discriminate unless the questions asked can be justified by some business purpose.

Therefore, inquiries about organizations, clubs, societies, and lodges of which an applicant may be a member or any other questions, which may indicate the applicant's race, sex, national origin, disability status, age, religion, color or ancestry if answered, should generally be avoided. Similarly, employers should not ask for a photograph of an applicant. If needed for identification purposes, a photograph may be obtained after an offer of employment is made and accepted.

2. Workplace Surveillance and Drug Testing

Public employers are generally limited to testing employees for drugs only if they have a "reasonable suspicion." The Fourth Amendment protects employees from unreasonable search and seizure and applies to public employers or private employers acting as instruments or agents of the government. Private employers are usually not subject to constitutional restraints in terms of drug testing, but may be affected by statute or the common law.

Employers must be careful to keep the results of drug and alcohol tests confidential and use extreme discretion when disciplining employees for drug or alcohol-related misconduct.

The Electronic Communications Privacy Act ("ECPA") prohibits private individuals and organizations (including employers) from intercepting wire or oral communications and sets out rules for tape recording telephone calls. It does allow a party to intercept a communication where one of the parties to the communication gives prior consent to such interception. An employer may also monitor employee conversations by listening in on an extension telephone if doing so is in the ordinary course of the employer's business. State wiretapping statutes may also provide even greater privacy protection for employees.

With respect to video surveillance, employers should be cautious of setting up video surveillance in areas of the workplace in which employees have reasonable expectations of privacy to avoid common law claims for invasion of privacy. These prohibited areas include bathrooms and locker rooms.

Employers should also consider informing employees of the possibility of video surveillance and document the need for such surveillance.

Courts have also generally upheld employers' interests in monitoring their employees' use of their computer systems, including email. The rationale for allowing employers to monitor computer activities is based on the fact that the corporation owns the computer. Employees therefore have neither a right nor an expectation of privacy in the computer-stored material. This rationale also applies to personal information stored on company-owned computers.

In order to protect themselves from constitutional and common law claims for invasion of privacy, many employers take steps to diminish an employee's expectation of privacy in their email communications by developing an email use policy and giving employees written notice of such a policy.

Employers may also have reason to search the workplace. For example, an employer may need to search for a file at an employee's desk, search to prevent the use or sale of drugs in the workplace, or search for weapons or other dangerous items. Again, the validity of the search will most likely be judged by balancing the employee's reasonable expectations of privacy in the area searched against the employer's legitimate interest in the search. More private areas, such as a locked drawer in a private office are likely to receive more protection than areas shared by multiple employees.

3. Post-Termination Activities

As previously mentioned, many terminated employees have filed claims for defamation and/or false light over the employer's release of information surrounding their termination. Therefore, employers must ensure that any information provided about a former employee is accurate. Most companies take a conservative approach and refuse to provide the reasons why the employment relationship ended and instead only provide more factual information, such as salary, start date, end date, and job title.

Another privacy issue that exists post-termination involves the release of any records or files related to the former employee. If a company retains files on former employees, the employer has an obligation to protect the former employees' personal information. As will be discussed in the next chapter, many states have data breach and notification laws that require a company to safeguard personal information and notify individuals affected by a data breach of the company's information technology systems.

Chapter 9: State Specific Privacy Laws

This chapter addresses state laws that regulate privacy in the United States. You should expect anywhere from 7 to 11 questions on your examination relating to state-specific privacy issues.

A. Glossary Terms

Your exam will contain a fair number of questions testing material from this chapter. Therefore, it is important that you read the definitions provided in the glossary for the few terms listed below. The glossary is located at:

http://www.cippexam.com/glossary

Glossary Terms: Breach Disclosure, Credit Freeze, Preemption, Protective Order, Redaction, Substitute Notice.

B. Overview of State Privacy Initiatives

So far, this book has predominantly focused on federal laws regulating privacy and only tangentially touched upon state-specific privacy initiatives, such as the California Online Privacy Protection Act ("CalOPPA").

It is important to remember that many federal privacy laws do not preempt states from enacting stricter laws in the same space. For example, under the Federal Wiretap Act, if one party to a communication consents to the interception, it is permitted. Under most analogous state laws, however, the consent of both parties is required. Therefore, in many instances, federal law only sets the floor of protection with state laws providing significant additional protection. For instance, several states explicitly recognize privacy as a fundamental right. For example, the Constitution of California provides each citizen with an "inalienable right" to pursue and obtain "privacy." Similarly, the Constitution of Alaska provides that "[t]he right of the people to privacy is recognized and shall not be infringed."

Three areas where virtually all states have enacted some form of legislation are (1) security breach notification, (2) data disposal, and (3) financial privacy, all of which are discussed in more detail below.

C. State Security Breach Notification Laws

Forty-seven states, the District of Columbia, Guam, Puerto Rico and the Virgin Islands have enacted legislation requiring private or government entities to notify individuals of security breaches of information involving personally identifiable information.

Security breach laws typically have provisions regarding who must comply with the law (typically, businesses, data/information brokers, or government entities); what constitutes a breach (generally, the unauthorized acquisition of computerized data); requirements for notice (for example, timing of method of notice and who must be notified); and exemptions that do not trigger notification (typically, when data is encrypted).

In 2003, California became the first state in the country to require notification of a security breach. California's security breach notification law has been used as a model for many other states and is therefore typical of many state's security breach notification laws.

California law requires a business or state agency to notify any California resident whose unencrypted personal information was acquired, or reasonably believed to have been acquired, by an unauthorized person. Therefore, as in initial matter, it is important to note that California's law applies only to unencrypted personal information. Encrypted personal information is exempt from the law.

In addition, the law applies to both business and state agencies. The authors of the California law stated that its intent was to give consumers an early warning that they were at risk of identity theft and fraud, so that they could take defensive action.

The type of personal information that triggers the requirement to notify individuals is "computerized data," consisting of an individual's name, plus one of the following: Social Security number; driver's license or California Identification Card number; financial account number, including credit or debit card number (along with any PIN or other access code where required for access to the account); medical information (any information regarding an individual's medical history, condition, or treatment); and health insurance information (policy or subscriber number or other identifier used by a health insurer, or information about an individual's application, claims history or appeals).

Notice must be given to individuals "in the most expedient time possible and without unreasonable delay." Notice to individuals may be delayed if a law enforcement agency determines that notification would impede a criminal investigation or in order to take measures necessary to determine the scope of the breach and restore reasonable integrity to the system. An entity that maintains the data but does not own it must notify the data owner immediately following discovery of a breach.

The notice to individuals must be written in plain language. It must include the name and contact information of the notifying entity, the types of personal information involved, contact information for the credit reporting agencies in the case of a breach of Social Security or driver's license numbers, and also, if known at the time of notification, the date of the breach, and a general description of the incident. Additional information that may be provided in the notice includes what the entity has done to protect individuals and advice on what individuals can do to protect themselves.

Since January 2012, organizations required to notify individuals of breaches affecting more than 500 Californians must submit a sample copy of the notice to the California Attorney General.

Any customer injured by a violation of the state's security breach notification law may institute a civil action to recover damages.

Since January 2015, California law also requires the source of the breach to provide appropriate identity theft prevention and mitigation services at no cost to the affected person for at least one year.

Some states extend the notification requirement for breaches involving paper records. These states include Alaska, Hawaii, Indiana, Iowa, Massachusetts, North Carolina, and Wisconsin. Most security breach notification laws, however, are restricted to electronic records, like California's law.

D. State Data Disposal Laws

Personal information is often collected by businesses and the government and stored in various formats, both digitally and on paper. At least 30 states have enacted laws that require entities to destroy, dispose of, or otherwise make personal information unreadable or undecipherable. Once again, California's law is discussed more fully below because it has been used as a template for many other states.

In accordance with California law, a business must take all reasonable steps to dispose of customer records within its custody by (a) shredding, (b) erasing, or (c) otherwise modifying the personal information in those records to make it unreadable or undecipherable through any means.

California's data disposal law uses the same definition of "personal information" as the state's security breach notification law (that is, name plus one other enumerated data element). Although the law does not set forth a specific time by which data must be destroyed, personal information should generally be destroyed once there is no longer any legitimate business need for retaining the information.

California's disposal rule is therefore similar to the Disposal Rule for consumer reports implemented as part of the Fair and Accurate Credit Transactions Act

("FACTA") because neither specifies a precise timeframe by which the data must be disposed.

E. State Financial Privacy Laws

Although the Fair Credit Reporting Act ("FCRA") generally preempts all state laws related to consumer reports, the same is not true for the privacy provisions of the Gramm-Leach-Bliley Act ("GLBA"). Therefore, states are free to enact consumer protection laws that are more protective than that of the GLBA. One such law is the California Financial Information Privacy Act (commonly referred to as "SB1").

SB1 was signed into law on August 27, 2003 and became effective on July 1, 2004. Although the overall structure of SB1 is similar to the privacy provisions of the GLBA, two important distinctions exist. First, SB1 requires opt-in notice before a financial institution can disclose customer information to nonaffiliated third parties for the marketing of non-financial products and services. The GLBA requires only opt-out notice in this situation.

Second, in accordance with SB1, privacy notices may be delivered electronically if they comply with the applicable provisions of the Electronic Signatures in Global and National Commerce Act ("ESIGN"). The GLBA requires that the initial and annual privacy notice be in writing (although the Consumer Financial Protection Bureau has recently proposed rules to allow financial institution to deliver privacy notices electronically under certain circumstances).

Violators of California's SB1 are subject to civil penalties of up to $2,500 per incident.

Conclusion for the CIPP/US Exam

Congratulations! You have completed the text portion of this study guide for the CIPP/US exam. The information you have just read was designed to provide you with the fundamentals of U.S. privacy law and introduce you to the concepts that will be tested on the CIPP/US exam. If you are new to the field of information privacy, we recommend that you read the text portion a second time to ensure that you have fully absorbed and understand the material.

The next section of this guide contains sample questions with detailed answers. The questions are designed to supplement the material contained in the text portion of this guide. Therefore, do not worry if some of the concepts are new to you. The sample questions are designed to teach you new material and not simply test your ability to remember the material presented in the beginning of this guide.

The questions below test facts that may appear on your exam. Thus, it is important that you carefully read both the questions and detailed answers provided. You will likely receive dozens of questions on your examination that test similar facts as our sample questions. If you answer these questions correctly, you are well on your way to passing the CIPP/US examination and becoming a certified privacy professional.

Sample Questions for the CIPP/US Exam

1. In accordance with the Fair Credit Reporting Act ("FCRA"), willful violations of the Act are punishable by a statutory maximum penalty of how much per violation?

    A. $500
    B. $2,000
    C. $2,500
    D. There is no limit

ANSWER: C. The FCRA provides a statutory penalty of up to $2,500 per violation for knowingly or willfully violating the Act. A consumer may recover his actual damages up to the statutory maximum, plus possible punitive damages, as well as reasonable attorney's fees and costs. Therefore, if this question was phrased differently and asked about the maximum penalty for a willful violation of the FCRA, the correct answer would be D because a consumer may recover punitive damages as well as actual damages. The statutory maximum, however, is $2,500.

2.   Which of the following may be classified as an
       unfair trade practice by the Federal Trade
       Commission ("FTC")?

   A.   A website's privacy notice clearly states that
          it will not encrypt sensitive personal
          information, and the website does not, in
          fact, encrypt the data
   B.   An organization promises to honor opt-out
          requests within 10 days but fails to honor
          opt-out requests
   C.   A rogue employee steals credit card
          information even though the organization
          took reasonable precautions to protect the
          credit card information
   D.   A federally insured bank does not comply
          with a regulation prohibiting the bank from
          revealing information about its customers

ANSWER: A. Section 5 of the FTC Act prohibits "unfair
or deceptive acts or practices in or affecting
commerce." Answer A is an example of an unfair
trade practice because the website is not being
deceptive, but the potential harm caused by the
website's failure to encrypt sensitive data clearly
outweighs the cost of providing encryption (a
commonplace and inexpensive security control).
Answer B is an example of a deceptive trade practice.
When companies tell consumers they will safeguard
their personal information, the FTC can and does take
law enforcement action to make sure that companies
live up to these promises. A violation of a promise
made in a privacy notice is an example of a deceptive
trade practice. Answer C would not be an unfair trade
practice because the organization has implemented
reasonable security measures, and the employee
simply committed a crime, which is generally

considered an unforeseeable event. Answer D is incorrect because the FTC does not have jurisdiction over banks and common carriers, which are under the supervision of other governmental agencies.

3.   In accordance with the Family Educational Rights and Privacy Act ("FERPA"), a school must provide parents or eligible students with their educational records within how many days of a request for the records?

   A.   10 days
   B.   30 days
   C.   45 days
   D.   90 days

ANSWER: C. Under FERPA, a school must provide a parent or eligible student with an opportunity to inspect and review the student's education records within 45 days following receipt of a request by the parent or eligible student.

4.   In accordance with the Fair Credit Reporting Act ("FCRA"), a consumer is entitled to a free copy of his credit report if he requests the report within how many days after an adverse action?

   A.   30 days
   B.   45 days
   C.   60 days
   D.   120 days

ANSWER: C. Each national consumer reporting agency that maintains a file on a consumer shall provide a free credit report to the consumer if, no later than 60 days after receipt by such consumer of an adverse action notification, the consumer makes a request for a copy of his credit report.

5.   In accordance with the Family Educational Rights and Privacy Act ("FERPA"), which of the following records does NOT constitute educational records?

   A.   Campus police records
   B.   School employment records
   C.   School discipline records
   D.   Educational transcripts

ANSWER: A. In 1992, FERPA was amended to exempt from the definition of educational records those records maintained by a law enforcement unit of the educational agency or institution. Educational records are defined in FERPA as "those records, files, documents, and other materials which (i) contain information directly related to a student and (ii) are maintained by an educational agency or institution or by a person acting for such agency or institution." School employment records, disciplinary records, and education transcripts are all forms of "educational records" under FERPA. Campus police records are not educational records under FERPA.

6.   Which agency is primarily responsible for protecting employee privacy in the United States?

A.   Federal Trade Commission ("FTC")
B.   Federal Communications Commission ("FCC")
C.   Federal Bureau of Investigation ("FBI")
D.   Office of Supervisory Jurisdiction ("OSJ")

ANSWER: A. The FTC is the agency primarily responsible for employee privacy in the United States. The FTC regulates unfair and deceptive commercial trade practices, as well as other laws protecting employee privacy, including the Fair Credit Reporting Act ("FCRA"), which regulates an employer's ability to obtain consumer reports for employment purposes. Other agencies responsible for employee privacy include the U.S. Equal Employment Opportunity Commission ("EEOC"), the Consumer Financial Protection Bureau ("CFPB"), and the National Labor Relations Board ("NLRB").

7.   The Federal Trade Commission ("FTC") was originally founded to enforce which body of law?

A.   Employee privacy
B.   Antitrust
C.   Tax and banking
D.   International trade

ANSWER: B. The FTC was created on September 26, 1914, when President Woodrow Wilson signed the Federal Trade Commission Act into law. The FTC opened its doors on March 16, 1915. The FTC's original mission was to enforce the rules of a competitive marketplace (that is, antitrust law).

Antitrust law promotes competition and protects consumers from anticompetitive mergers and business practices.

8. The Children's Online Privacy Protection Act ("COPPA") was enacted to primarily prevent which of the following activities?

    A. To prevent children from using a parent's credit card information without consent
    B. To protect the privacy of children under 18 years of age
    C. To protect children from malicious or abusive users of interactive online services
    D. To educate parents about the danger of the Internet

ANSWER: C. COPPA prohibits unfair and deceptive acts or practices in connection with the collection, use, or disclosure of personal information from children under the age of 13 in an online environment. The Act was passed in response to an alarming trend of children posting their personal information in interactive public areas, such as chat rooms and bulletin boards, which were accessible to all online users.

9.   Which of the following companies allegedly committed an unfair trade practice by retroactively changing their privacy policy to permit the sharing of personal information without notifying its users?

    A.   Microsoft
    B.   Eli Lilly
    C.   Google
    D.   Gateway Learning

ANSWER: D. In 2004, the FTC filed a complaint against Gateway Learning Corp. for, in part, retroactively revising its privacy policy to permit sharing of its users' personal information. Gateway Learning subsequently settled the matter with the FTC and in a consent decree agreed not to sell, rent, or loan to third parties its users' personal information.

10.   The following fact pattern applies to questions 10 – 14.

Katie goes to her neighborhood pharmacy to fill her prescription for heart medication. When asked, Katie hands the pharmacist her prescription and insurance identification card. The pharmacist provides Katie with the proper dose and type of medication as indicated on the prescription but inadvertently forgets to give Katie back her insurance identification card. One week later, Natalie, another patron of the pharmacy, finds Katie's insurance identification card in her medication bag, calls the pharmacy using the contact number posted on the pharmacy's website, and returns the insurance identification card to the

pharmacy. The pharmacy promptly returns the card to Katie the next business day.
Has a violation of the Health Insurance Portability and Accountability Act ("HIPAA") occurred?

A. No, the insurance identification card was safely returned to its owner within a reasonable amount of time
B. No, the insurance identification card does not constitute protected health information
C. No, the pharmacy is not a covered entity
D. Yes, the insurance identification card constitutes protected health information and the loss of the card created a significant risk of harm to the patient

ANSWER: D. Pharmacies are classified as healthcare providers under HIPAA and therefore are covered entities. The insurance identification card also constitutes protected health information because it relates to the provision of healthcare to an individual. In accordance with HIPAA, a data breach is, generally speaking, an impermissible use or disclosure under the Privacy Rule that compromises the security or privacy of protected health information. The Privacy Rule pertains to all forms of PHI, including both paper and electronic records. Therefore, the incident constitutes a data breach under HIPAA.

11. Did the pharmacy commit a violation of HIPAA's Privacy Rule?

    A.   No, the insurance identification card does not constitute protected health information

    B.   No, the insurance identification card was disclosed in connection with treatment, payment, or health care operations

    C.   No, the pharmacy has implicit authorization to use the insurance identification card

    D.   Yes, the insurance identification card constitutes protected health information, and the card was disclosed to a third party without Katie's authorization

ANSWER: D. Under the Privacy Rule, covered entities may only disclose PHI to facilitate treatment, payment, or healthcare operations without a patient's express written authorization. Any other disclosure of PHI requires the covered entity to obtain written authorization from the data subject for the disclosure. The Privacy Rule pertains to all forms of PHI, including both paper and electronic records. Therefore, a violation has occurred.

12. Which of the following is required of the pharmacy by the Health Insurance Portability and Accountability Act ("HIPAA")?

A. The pharmacy must have a notice on its website informing customers about how they may file a complaint with the Office for Civil Rights ("OCR") at the Department of Health and Human Services ("HHS")

B. The pharmacy must encrypt all protected health information

C. The pharmacy must notify Katie within 10 business days of the data breach

D. The pharmacy must report the data breach to secretary of the HHS within 60 days of discovery of the breach

ANSWER: A. The pharmacy is a covered entity, and a covered entity must prominently post and make available its notice on any website it maintains that provides information about its customer services or benefits. HIPAA complaints should be lodged with the Office for Civil Rights at the Department of Health and Human Services. The pharmacy must also notify Katie of the breach. This individual notification must be provided without unreasonable delay and in no case later than 60 days following the discovery of the breach and must include, to the extent possible, (1) a brief description of the breach, (2) a description of the types of information that were involved in the breach, (3) the steps affected individuals should take to protect themselves from potential harm, (4) a brief description of what the covered entity is doing to investigate the breach, mitigate the harm, and prevent further breaches, and (5) contact information for the pharmacy. Covered entities that experience a breach affecting more than 500 residents of a state or jurisdiction are, in addition to notifying the affected individuals, required to provide notice to prominent media outlets serving the state or jurisdiction. In addition to notifying affected individuals and the media (where appropriate), covered entities must notify the Secretary of HSS regardless of the size of the breach. If the breach affects 500 or more individuals, covered entities must notify the Secretary without unreasonable delay and in no case later than 60 days following the breach. If, however, a breach affects fewer than 500 individuals, as occurred with Katie's insurance identification card, the covered entity only needs to notify the Secretary of such breaches on an annual basis.

13.   If a user of a consumer report takes adverse action against a consumer based on information contained in the consumer report, which of the following does NOT need to be disclosed to the consumer?

   A.   The name, address, and telephone number of the consumer reporting agency that provided the consumer report
   B.   A statement explaining to the consumer that he has the right to obtain a copy of the consumer report free of charge from the consumer reporting agency
   C.   An explanation of the technical safeguards instituted by the consumer reporting agency that protect the consumer's confidential information
   D.   A statement advising the consumer of his right to dispute the accuracy or completeness of the consumer report with the consumer reporting agency

ANSWER: C. If a user takes adverse action against a consumer based on information contained in a consumer report, the user must provide notice to the consumer. The notice must include (1) the name, address, and telephone number of the consumer reporting agency that provided the consumer report, (2) a statement explaining to the consumer that he has the right to obtain a copy of the consumer report free of charge from the consumer reporting agency, and (3) a statement advising the consumer of his right to dispute the accuracy or completeness of the consumer report with the consumer reporting agency.

14. If an information technology auditor working on behalf of a hospital inadvertently loses the unencrypted medical billing records of 400 individuals, what type of notification is NOT required?

A. The hospital must provide notice to prominent media outlets serving the state or jurisdiction
B. The hospital or auditor must provide individual notice to the affected individuals
C. The hospital must notify the Secretary of the Department of Health and Human Services ("HHS")
D. The auditor must notify the hospital following discovery of the breach

ANSWER: A. In accordance with the Health Information Technology for Economic and Clinical Health ("HITECH") Act, a covered entity or its business associates must provide individual notification following a breach of unsecured protected health information. A "business associate" is a person or entity that performs certain functions or activities that involve the use or disclosure of protected health information on behalf of, or provides services to, a covered entity. Therefore, an information technology auditor working on behalf of a medical billing company is a business associate of the medical billing company. Notice to the media is only required for breaches affecting more than 500 residents of a state or jurisdiction. With respect to a breach at or by a business associate, while the covered entity is ultimately responsible for ensuring individuals are notified, the covered entity may delegate the responsibility of providing individual notice to the business associate. The covered entity and business associate should consider which entity is in the best position to provide notice to the individual, which may depend on various circumstances, such as the functions the business associate performs on behalf of the covered entity and which entity has the relationship with the affected individuals.

15.   The National Do Not Call Registry is primarily enforced by which two entities?

A.   Department of Transportation and the FTC
B.   U.S. Department of Justice and the FTC
C.   Department of Commerce and the FCC
D.   The FTC and FCC

ANSWER: D. Pursuant to its authority under the Telephone Consumer Protection Act ("TCPA"), the Federal Communication Commission ("FCC") established, together with the Federal Trade Commission ("FTC"), a national Do Not Call Registry in 2003. The registry is nationwide in scope, applies to all telemarketers (with the exception of certain non-profit organizations), and covers both interstate and intrastate telemarketing calls. Commercial telemarketers are not allowed to call you if your number is on the registry, subject to certain exceptions. The FTC and FCC are the primary enforcers of the National Do Not Call Registry.

16. Which of the following occurred as a result of Health Information Technology for Economic and Clinical Health ("HITECH") Act?

   A. Covered entities were required to enter into written contracts with business associates ensuring privacy and security of protected health information
   B. The HIPAA Security Rule was extended to business associates of covered entities
   C. Covered entities were required to take reasonable steps to limit the use or disclosure of, and requests for, protected health information to the minimum necessary to accomplish the intended purpose
   D. Covered entities were required to take appropriate administrative, physical and technical safeguards to ensure the confidentiality, integrity, and security of electronic protected health information

ANSWER: B. HITECH extended the HIPAA Security Rule to business associates of covered entities. Previously, privacy and security requirements were imposed on business associates through contractual agreements with covered entities. HITECH made business associates directly responsible for complying with the Security Rule. The HIPAA Security Rule establishes national standards to protect individuals' electronic personal health information that is created, received, used, or maintained by a covered entity or business associate of a covered entity. The Security Rule requires appropriate administrative, physical, and technical safeguards to ensure the confidentiality, integrity, and security of electronic protected health information.

17. In accordance with the Fair Credit Reporting Act ("FCRA"), willful disclosure of financial information in violation of the Act is punishable by a penalty of how much?

A. $500
B. $2,000
C. $2,500
D. There is no limit

ANSWER: D. For willful violations of the FCRA, a consumer may recover his actual damages up to the statutory maximum of $2,500, plus possible punitive damages, as well as reasonable attorney's fees and costs. Therefore, the correct answer is D because a consumer may recover his actual damages and punitive damages. The FCRA provides a statutory maximum penalty for actual damages of up to $2,500 per violation for knowingly or willfully violating the Act. However, this question was not limited to actual damages.

18. Which of the following practices was NOT implemented by the Fair and Accurate Credit Transactions Act ("FACTA")?

A. Consumers have the right to obtain one free copy of their credit report from each of the three major national credit bureaus every 12 months

B. Merchants may print the first 4 digits of a credit card number on a receipt

C. Implemented the Disposal Rule to ensure that proper disposal of information in consumer reports and records are protected against unauthorized access to or use of the information.

D. Implemented the Red Flags Rule to help combat identity theft

ANSWER: B. FACTA provides that "no person that accepts credit cards or debit cards for the transaction of business shall print more than the last 5 digits of the card number or the expiration date upon any receipt provided to the cardholder at the point of the sale or transaction." Therefore, the first four digits of the card number may not be printed. In accordance with FACTA, consumers have the right to obtain one free copy of their credit report from each national credit bureau every 12 months. FACTA also implemented the Disposal Rule and Red Flags Rule.

19. When an employer obtains an investigative consumer report on an employee suspected of misconduct, which of the following is required?

A. The employer must provide advance notice of the investigation to the employee

B. The employer must provide a summary of the nature and scope of the investigation if adverse action is taken as a result of the investigation

C. The employer must obtain the employee's consent to the investigation

D. The employer must certify to the consumer reporting agency that the necessary notices have been provided to the employee

ANSWER: B. The Fair Credit Reporting Act ("FCRA") was amended in 2003 to exempt investigative consumer reports related to suspected employee misconduct from many of the requirements of the FCRA, including consent, advanced notice, and certification. The employer is still required, however, to provide a summary of the nature and scope of the investigation if adverse action is taken as a result of the investigation.

20. Which of the following is NOT a requirement of the Fair Credit Reporting Act ("FCRA")?

A. Consumer reporting agencies furnish consumer reports only to persons having a permissible purpose

B. Users of consumer reports certify to the consumer reporting agency their permissible purpose and also certify that the information contained in the consumer report will not be used for any other purpose

C. State consumer reporting agencies must provide consumers with a free copy of their credit report every year

D. If a user takes any adverse action based on information contained in a consumer report, the user must provide notice of the adverse action to the consumer

ANSWER: C. Every national consumer reporting agency that maintains a file on a consumer shall provide a free credit report to the consumer if, no later than 60 days after receipt by such consumer of an adverse action notification, the consumer makes a request for a copy of his credit report. The free credit report provision applies only to national consumer reporting agencies (such as Experian, TransUnion, and Equifax) and not local or state consumer reporting agencies.

21.   In accordance with the Bank Secrecy Act, under which circumstance must a financial institution file a suspicious activity report?

   A.   When the bank detects a suspicious transaction of $25,000 even if the bank does not know the identity of the perpetrator
   B.   For all transactions over $10,000
   C.   For all transactions over $5,000
   D.   When the bank detects a suspicious cash transaction of $1,000 coupled with a credit transaction of $3,000

ANSWER: A. The Bank Secrecy Act of 1970, also known as the Currency and Foreign Transactions Reporting Act, requires financial institutions in the United States to assist government agencies to detect and prevent money laundering. Specifically, the Act requires financial institutions to keep records of cash purchases of negotiable instruments, file reports of cash purchases of these negotiable instruments of more than $10,000 (daily aggregate amount), and report suspicious activity that might signify money laundering, tax evasion, or other criminal activities. Currency Transaction Reports ("CTRs") and Suspicious Activity Reports ("SARs") are the primary means used by banks to satisfy the requirements of the BSA. A SAR must be filed when a bank detects a suspicious transaction of $25,000 or more even if the identity of the perpetrator is unknown. A SAR must also be filed when a bank detects a suspicious currency transaction of $5,000 or more.

22. Which of the following states have a data breach notification law that mandates the notice contain the approximate date of the breach?

A. Massachusetts
B. California
C. Oregon
D. New York

ANSWER: C. Oregon Rev. Stat. § 646A.604 requires that notice of a data breach include (1) a description of the incident in general terms; (2) the approximate date of the breach of security; (3) the type of personal information obtained as a result of the breach of security; (4) contact information of the person responsible for the breach; (5) contact information for national consumer reporting agencies; and (6) advice to the consumer to report suspected identity theft to law enforcement and the Federal Trade Commission ("FTC").

23. Which of the following cannot be included in the notification letter to affected residents after discovery of a data breach in accordance with Massachusetts law?

A. Information about the consumer's right to obtain a police report
B. Information on how the affected individual can obtain a credit freeze
C. The number of residents affected by the breach
D. Contact information for national consumer reporting agencies

ANSWER: C. Mass. Gen. Laws § 93H-3 requires that the notice provided after a data breach must include (1) the consumer's right to obtain a police report and (2) how a consumer requests a security freeze and the necessary information to be provided when requesting the security freeze, and any fees required to be paid to any of the consumer reporting agencies. The notification cannot include the nature of the breach or the number of residents affected by the breach. Other information, such as contact information for national consumer reporting agencies, may also be optionally provided in the notice.

24. When a website operator states in its privacy notice that it will not share financial information with third parties and then shares financial information with a third-party affiliate, what recourse may occur?

    A. The FTC may bring an action against the operator for unfair competition

    B. The FTC may bring an action against the operator for a deceptive trade practice

    C. A user of the website may bring a criminal complaint against the operator

    D. The FTC may bring an action under Section 7 of the FTC Act

ANSWER: B. If an organization fails to comply with its privacy notice, it may be held liable by the FTC for a deceptive trade practice under Section 5 of the FTC Act, which prohibits "unfair or deceptive acts or practices in or affecting commerce." When companies tell consumers they will safeguard their personal information, the FTC can and does take law enforcement action to make sure that companies live up to these promises. A violation of a promise made in a privacy notice is an example of a deceptive trade practice. The distinction between a deceptive trade practice and an unfair trade practice is often tested on the CIPP/US exam.

25. The Children's Online Privacy Protection Act ("COPPA") applies to whom?

A. Operators of websites soliciting business in the United States
B. Operators of websites soliciting financial information from customers in the United States
C. Operators of commercial websites that are directed to children under 13 years of age
D. Operators of commercial websites that are directed to children under 18 years of age

ANSWER: C. COPPA was enacted in 1998 to curtail the collection of personal information from children. The Act applies to websites and online services operated for commercial purposes that are directed to children under the age of 13. In addition, the Act applies to operators having actual knowledge that children under 13 are providing information online. In addition to requiring operators of these websites to conspicuously post a privacy notice, COPPA also requires that website operators obtain verifiable parental consent prior to any collection, use, or disclosure of personal information from persons under the age of 13.

26. The Gramm-Leach-Bliley Act ("GLBA") applies to which organizations?

A. All organizations that process financial data
B. Financial organizations with more than 10,000 customers
C. All organizations regulated by the Department of Commerce
D. Domestic financial institutions

ANSWER: D. The GLBA, also known as the "Financial Services Modernization Act," was enacted in 1999. It applies to institutions that are significantly engaged in financial activities in the United States (also known as "domestic financial institutions"). The GLBA requires domestic financial institutions to, among other things, provide an initial privacy notice when the customer relationship is established (and annually thereafter) and also provide opt-out notice prior to sharing non-public personal information with non-affiliated third parties.

27. What is the main purpose of the Fair Credit Reporting Act ("FCRA")?

A. Enable data reporters to efficiently report valid debts on a consumer's credit report
B. Allow employers to quickly access financial data of their employees
C. Increase the ability of the government to access consumer reports of suspected criminals
D. Increase the accuracy and fairness of credit reporting and limit the use of consumer reports to permissible purposes

ANSWER: D. The FCRA was originally enacted in 1970 and more recently was updated by the Fair and Accurate Credit Transactions Act of 2003 ("FACTA"). The FCRA applies to consumer reporting agencies ("CRAs"), such as Experian, TransUnion, and Equifax, and to users of consumer reports. The main purpose of the FCRA was to increase the accuracy and fairness of credit reporting and limit the use of consumer reports to permissible purposes, such as for employment reasons and the underwriting of insurance.

28.   What is the basic rule for processing protected health information under the Health Insurance Portability and Accountability Act ("HIPAA")?

A.   Patients must opt in before their protected health information is shared with other organizations unless the purpose is for treatment, payment, or healthcare operations

B.   Patients must opt out to prevent their protected health information from being shared with other organizations unless the purpose is for treatment, payment, or healthcare operations

C.   Processing of protected health information is prohibited for all purposes without opt-in consent

D.   Processing of protected health information is prohibited for all purposes without opt-out consent

ANSWER: A. Under HIPAA's Privacy Rule, covered entities may disclose protected heath information ("PHI") to facilitate treatment, payment, or health care operations without a patient's express written authorization. Any other disclosure of PHI requires the covered entity to obtain written authorization from the data subject for the disclosure (that is, opt-in consent). In addition, when a covered entity discloses PHI, it must also make reasonable efforts to disclose only the minimum information necessary to achieve its purpose.

29. In accordance with the Health Insurance Portability and Accountability Act ("HIPAA"), the Department of Health and Human Services ("HHS") has promulgated which of the following rules to address the handling of protected health information?

   A. Transaction Rule and Equal Access Rule
   B. Privacy Rule and the Security Rule
   C. Privacy Rule and Equal Access Rule
   D. Security Rule and the Notification Rule

ANSWER: B. HIPAA was enacted in 1996 to define policies, procedures, and guidelines that covered entities must follow for maintaining the privacy and security of individually identifiable protected health information ("PHI"). Covered entities generally include healthcare clearinghouses, employer sponsored health plans, health insurers, and healthcare providers. As directed by Title II of HIPAA, the Department of Health and Human Services ("HHS") has promulgated two important rules to address the handling of PHI: (1) the Privacy Rule and (2) the Security Rule.

30. California's security breach notification law requires which entities to disclose a breach of security of unencrypted personal information to California residents?

A. Only companies physically located in California
B. Only state agencies
C. Only companies that conduct business in California
D. All state agencies and companies that conduct business in California

ANSWER: D. California's security breach notification law (S.B. 1386) requires a state agency, or a person or business that conducts business in California, to disclose in specified ways any breach of the security of data to any resident of California whose unencrypted personal information was, or is reasonably believed to have been, acquired by an unauthorized person.

31. Which of the following strategies will prevent a company from having to notify residents of a data breach involving personal information?

A. Encrypt all personal information, including sensitive personal information
B. Ensure that all personal information is protected by adequate safeguards
C. Use a firewall to protect all personal information
D. Purge all personal information after one year

ANSWER: A. Virtually all state security breach notification laws exempt encrypted personal information. Therefore, if a company encrypts all personal information, it will not have to notify residents even if there is a security breach. Although the other strategies may help reduce an organization's risk of a security breach, if a breach of unencrypted personal information does occur, the organization will still be required to notify the affected residents.

32.   The Disposal Rule contained in the Fair and Accurate Credit Transactions Act ("FACTA") applies to which type of documents?

   A.   Educational records
   B.   Financial data
   C.   Consumer reports and records
   D.   Employee evaluations

ANSWER: C. Any business or individual who uses a consumer report for a business purpose is subject to the requirements of the Disposal Rule. The Rule requires the proper disposal of information in consumer reports and records to protect against unauthorized access to or use of the information. The standard for the proper disposal of information derived from a consumer report is flexible, and allows the organizations and individuals covered by the Rule to determine what measures are reasonable based on the sensitivity of the information, the costs and benefits of different disposal methods, and changes in technology. The Disposal Rule applies to consumer reports or information derived from consumer reports. The Fair Credit Reporting Act ("FCRA") defines the term consumer report to include information obtained from a consumer reporting company that is used – or expected to be used – in establishing a consumer's eligibility for credit, employment, or insurance, among other purposes. Credit reports and credit scores are types of consumer reports. Reports that businesses or individuals receive with information relating to employment background, check writing history, insurance claims, residential or tenant history, or medical history are also considered consumer reports.

33. Which of the following statements accurately describe National Security Letters ("NSLs")?

A. They may only be issued by officials in FBI headquarters
B. They may only request information pertaining to a foreign power or the agent of a foreign power
C. They do not require prior judicial authorization
D. They may not contain nondisclosure provisions prohibiting the recipient from disclosing the contents of the letter

ANSWER: C. A national security letter ("NSL") is an administrative subpoena issued by the Federal Bureau of Investigation ("FBI") in an authorized national security investigation "to protect against international terrorism or clandestine intelligence activities." The USA PATRIOT Act made several changes to NSL practice, including (1) expanding issuing authority beyond FBI headquarter officials to include the heads of the FBI field offices, also known as Special Agents in Charge ("SACs"); (2) eliminated the requirement that the record information sought pertain to a foreign power or the agent of a foreign power; (3) required instead that the NSL request be relevant to an investigation to protect against international terrorism or foreign spying; and (4) added the caveat that no such investigation of an American can be predicated exclusively on First Amendment-protected activities. The FBI may issue NSLs without obtaining prior judicial authorization. NSLs may also contain a nondisclosure provision preventing the recipient from revealing the contents of the NSL or even that fact that it was received. The nondisclosure provision is intended to prevent the recipient of an NSL from compromising an FBI investigation.

34. Which of the following is NOT a source of American law?

   A.   Regulatory bodies
   B.   Legislature
   C.   Common law
   D.   Court decisions

ANSWER: C. In the United States, law is derived from various sources. The legislature (that is, Congress) creates statutory law. Regulatory bodies and administrative agencies, such as the Federal Trade Commission ("FTC") and Federal Communication Commission ("FCC"), create administrative law. Court decisions are the basis of common law (also sometimes referred to as "case law"). Therefore, regulatory bodies, the legislature, and court decisions are all primary sources of American law. Common law, on the other hand, is a type of law and not a source of law. Common law is the class of law developed by judges through decisions of courts and similar tribunals, as opposed to statutes adopted through the legislative process or regulations issued by the executive branch.

35. The Communications Assistance for Law Enforcement Act ("CALEA") requires telecommunication providers to do which of the following?

   A. Design their equipment and services to enable law enforcement officials to conduct electronic surveillance
   B. Monitor their customers for suspicious activity
   C. Report suspicious activity to law enforcement
   D. Protect children under the age of 13 by prohibiting users from collecting personal information related to children

ANSWER: A. In response to concerns that emerging technologies, such as digital and wireless communications, were making it increasingly difficult for law enforcement agencies to execute authorized surveillance, Congress enacted the Communications Assistance for Law Enforcement Act ("CALEA") in 1994. CALEA requires telecommunications carriers to ensure that their equipment, facilities, and services are designed so that enforcement officials can conduct electronic surveillance pursuant to a court order or other lawful authorization.

36. When interviewing an applicant for an open position, an organization may ask which of the following questions without violating antidiscrimination laws?

A. If the applicant is currently using illegal drugs
B. If the applicant was born in the United States
C. If there are any religious holidays that the candidate will need to take off from work if hired
D. If the applicant is married

ANSWER: A. When conducting employment interviews, organizations should refrain from asking questions that may reveal whether the applicant is a member of a protected class. Therefore, questions that may reveal race, religion, sexual orientation, or national origin should be avoided. An organization may, however, ask an applicant about current illegal drug use as long as the question does not implicate drug addiction, which may be viewed as a disability. Questions about marital status and number and ages of children are frequently used to discriminate against women and may violate Title VII if used to deny or limit employment opportunities.

37. Which of the following is considered a best practice when an organization is considering posting employee photographs on its internal intranet website?

A. Process all employee requests to take down their photograph within 5 business days of receiving the request
B. Require written consent from employees after posting their photographs
C. Request a photograph from each employee before the employee is hired and obtain consent for posting the photograph in the employment agreement
D. Obtain the employee's consent before posting the photograph

ANSWER: D. When an organization posts an employee's photograph on its internal intranet or public website, it should first obtain consent from the employee. In fact, in Europe, prior consent for the use of photographs (even on security badges) is always required. Organizations should not request an applicant to submit a photograph before being hired because the photograph may reveal membership in a protected class, thereby potentially resulting in an antidiscrimination claim by the applicant.

38. Which of the following accurately describes an employer's ability to conduct video surveillance of its employees?

A. Employers may conduct video surveillance of their employees as long as the employer has a legitimate business interest in the surveillance

B. Employers may never conduct video surveillance of their employees because it constitutes an invasion of privacy

C. Employers may conduct video surveillance of their employees after obtaining consent from the manager of the employees

D. Employers may generally conduct video surveillance of their employees as long as the surveillance is not in a private place where employees have an expectation of privacy

ANSWER: D. With respect to video surveillance, employers should be cautious of setting up video surveillance in areas of the workplace in which employees have a reasonable expectation of privacy. These private areas include bathrooms and locker rooms. Employers should also consider informing employees of the possibility of video surveillance and document the need for such surveillance.

39. Which of the following is considered a best practice after terminating an employee?

A. The employer should allow the employee a minimum of two weeks to collect his belongings and return all corporate assets

B. The employer should restrict or terminate the employee's access to the company's informational assets and collect all computing devices storing company information, including personal information

C. The employer should immediately change all administrator passwords and delete the employee's user account

D. The employer should forward all mail directed to the former employee to the former employee's new mailing address

ANSWER: B. After termination of an employee, an employer should take steps to ensure that the organization's informational and physical assets are protected. Generally, the employee's access to such assets should be restricted or removed, and the organization should collect devices containing company information, including personal information. In most cases, the former employee's access should be terminated immediately. The organization should also remind the former employee of his obligation not to inappropriately exploit company data. Although personal mail addressed to the former employee should be forwarded to his new mailing address, work-related messages should be reviewed because they may contain proprietary information that the former employee is no longer authorized to access.

40. The following fact pattern applies to questions 40 and 41.

ABC Corporation is a financial institution that partners with third-party affiliate wine companies to market and sell high-end wine and spirits on a monthly subscription basis. ABC obtains credit reports on consumers from consumer reporting agencies and stores the credit reports in a database. The database is accessible by the wine companies, which use the information contained in the credit report, including monthly income and credit history, to determine if a particular consumer is eligible to join the program. If eligible, the consumer is sent an informational kit describing the program with an application form.

What must the affiliate wine companies do before using the information contained in the credit reports for marketing purposes?

A. Obtain prior written authorization from the consumers
B. Provide opt-out notice to the consumers
C. Provide a copy of the reports to the consumers
D. Certify to the credit reporting agency that furnished the reports that it is has a permissible purpose

ANSWER: B. The Fair and Accurate Credit Transactions Act ("FACTA") imposes obligations on consumer reporting agencies, as well as users and furnishers of consumer reports. The Act prohibits an affiliate that receives eligibility information from using that information to make a solicitation for marketing purposes unless (1) the consumer receives notice, (2) has a reasonable opportunity and simple method to opt out of such solicitations, and (3) the consumer does not opt out.

41. If ABC plans on taking an adverse action against a consumer based on information in his credit report, what must it do before taking the adverse action?

   A. Provide a complete copy of the underwriting file to the consumer
   B. Provide a complete copy of the credit report to the consumer
   C. Provide notice of the adverse action to the consumer; disclose the name, address, and telephone number of the consumer reporting agency furnishing the credit report; and notify the consumer about his right to obtain a free copy of his consumer report from the consumer reporting agency
   D. Allow the consumer to opt-out of future marketing mailings from ABC or its affiliates

ANSWER: C. In accordance with the Fair Credit Reporting Act ("FCRA"), users of consumer reports have several responsibilities. If a user takes any adverse action with respect to any consumer that is based in whole or in part on any information contained in a consumer report, the user must (1) provide notice of the adverse action to the consumer, (2) disclose the name, address, and telephone number of the consumer reporting agency furnishing the information to the user, and (3) notify the consumer about his right to obtain a free copy of his consumer report from the consumer reporting agency and how to dispute inaccurate or incomplete information in the report. A copy of the report is required to be provided only when taking an adverse action for employment purposes. Therefore, ABC does not need to provide a copy of the report to the consumer because the adverse action is not related to employment. If an employer uses a consumer report to take an adverse action against a potential or current employee, the employer must provide a copy of the report to the employee.

42. Which of the following companies was directed by the Federal Trade Commission ("FTC") to implement a comprehensive information security program for allegedly carrying out a deceptive trade practice with respect to its Passport web service?

   A.   Google
   B.   Microsoft
   C.   Gateway Learning
   D.   GeoCities

ANSWER: B. In 2002, Microsoft agreed to settle FTC charges concerning the privacy and security of information collected through its Passport web service. Microsoft's privacy policy claimed, among other things, that Passport "achieves a high level of Web Security by using technologies and systems designed to prevent unauthorized access to your personal information." The FTC alleged that Microsoft misrepresented the level of security provided by the Passport service. As part of the consent order, Microsoft agreed to establish and maintain a comprehensive information security program reasonably designed to protect the security, confidentiality, and integrity of personal information collected from or about its consumers.

43.   Common law is derived from which of the following?

A.   Statutes created by the legislature
B.   The United States Constitution
C.   Societal customs and expectations
D.   Executive orders

ANSWER: C. Common law is developed by judges through decisions of courts (called "case law"), as opposed to statutes adopted through the legislative process or regulations issued by the executive branch. Common law is based on societal customs and expectations.

44.   Which of the following agencies does NOT presently have the power to issue regulations related to consumer privacy?

A.   Office of the Comptroller of Currency ("OCC")
B.   Federal Trade Commission ("FTC")
C.   Consumer Financial Protection Board ("CFPB")
D.   Federal Communication Commission ("FCC")

ANSWER: A. The OCC charters, regulates, and supervises all national banks and federal savings associations, as well as federal branches and agencies of foreign banks. The OCC is an independent bureau of the U.S. Department of the Treasury. On July 21, 2011, the OCC removed all regulations relating to privacy of consumer financial information and transferred its rulemaking authority in this area to the Consumer Financial Protection Bureau ("CFPB") pursuant to Title X of the Dodd-Frank Wall Street Reform and Consumer Protection Act.

45.   The Red Flags Rule is designed to combat what type of activity?

A.   Acquisition of personal information from minors
B.   Identify theft
C.   Inappropriate disclosure of financial information
D.   Transfer of personal information out of the United States

ANSWER: B. The Fair and Accurate Credit Transactions Act ("FACTA") provides a Red Flags Rule designed to combat identify theft. Identity theft refers to a fraud committed or attempted using the identifying information of another person without authority. The Red Flags Rule requires creditors and financial institutions to address the risk of identity theft by developing and implementing written identity theft prevention programs to help identify, detect, and respond to patterns, practices, or specific activities – known as "red flags" – that could indicate identity theft.

46. In accordance with the Electronic Communications Privacy Act ("ECPA"), when may a person lawfully monitor another's telephone call?

A. Only when both parties to the call have given their consent
B. Monitoring telephones call is illegal under all circumstances
C. Ten days after providing notice of the monitoring to both parties of the call
D. When one of the parties to the call has given his consent

ANSWER: D. The Electronic Communications Privacy Act ("ECPA") was enacted in 1986 to update the Federal Wiretap Act. The ECPA protects wire, oral, and electronic communications while those communications are being made, are in transit, and when they are stored on computers. Therefore, ECPA applies to email, telephone conversations, and data stored electronically. Two notable exceptions to ECPA's broad prohibition against interception of communications exist. First, under federal law, if one party to the communication consents to the interception, it is permitted. Under most state laws, however, consent of both parties is required. Second, operators are authorized to intercept and monitor communications placed over their facilities in order to combat fraud and theft of service. Because this question specifically deals with the federal law (ECPA) and not state law, the correct answer is that only one party to the call needs to consent to the interception.

47. The Do Not Call Registry applies to what type of marketing?

A. Email marketing
B. Unsolicited commercial messages
C. Telemarketing
D. Online marketing

ANSWER: C. Pursuant to its authority under the Telephone Consumer Protection Act ("TCPA"), the Federal Communication Commission ("FCC") established, together with the Federal Trade Commission ("FTC"), a national Do Not Call Registry in 2003. The registry is nationwide in scope, applies to all telemarketers (with the exception of certain non-profit organizations), and covers both interstate and intrastate telemarketing calls. Commercial telemarketers are not allowed to call you if your number is on the registry, subject to certain exceptions.

48. What is the original purpose of bank secrecy laws?

A. To enable banks to better share information
B. To protect customer's personal and financial information
C. To permit access of financial data by government authorities for national security purposes
D. To ensure creditors have appropriate access to a debtor's financial information

ANSWER: B. Bank secrecy is a legal principle in some jurisdictions under which banks are not allowed to provide to authorities personal and account information about their customers unless certain conditions apply (for example, a criminal complaint has been filed). Bank secrecy laws are routinely criticized because they may enable money laundering.

49. Which of the following correctly describes the Gramm-Leach-Bliley Act ("GLBA")?

A. The Act is based on the permissible purpose approach to privacy
B. The Act covers all financial information, including publicly available information
C. The Act requires opt-in consent when sharing financial information with unaffiliated third parties
D. The Act establishes a complicated set of privacy and security requirements for domestic financial institutions

ANSWER: D. GLBA is based on the fair information practices approach to privacy and not the permissible purpose approach. GLBA also does not cover publicly available information, and the sharing of financial data with unaffiliated third parties is permitted with opt-out consent. The GLBA sets forth two important rules that domestic financial institutions must adhere to: (1) the Privacy Rule and (2) the Safeguards Rule. Therefore, D is the best answer.

50. Which of the following is NOT exempt from disclosure under the Freedom of Information Act ("FOIA")?

A. Records containing trade secrets
B. Records containing the location of oil wells
C. Records describing the data handling practices of financial institutions
D. Records pertaining to federal regulatory agencies, federal employees, and federal agents

ANSWER: D. FOIA has the following nine exemptions: (1) those documents properly classified as secret in the interest of national defense or foreign policy; (2) documents related solely to internal personnel rules and practices; (3) documents specifically exempted by other statutes; (4) a trade secret or privileged or confidential commercial or financial information obtained from a person; (5) a privileged inter-agency or intra-agency memorandum or letter; (6) a personnel, medical, or similar file the release of which would constitute a clearly unwarranted invasion of personal privacy; (7) documents compiled for law enforcement purposes; (8) records contained in or related to examination, operating, or condition reports about financial institutions; and (9) those documents containing exempt information (for example, the location) about gas or oil wells. Answers A, B, and C fall in exemptions (4), (9), and (8), respectively. Answer D is not a recognized exemption and, therefore, is the correct answer.

51.   The Children's Online Privacy Protection Act ("COPPA") prevents website operators from performing which of the following activities?

A.   Creating a website with content designed for children under 13 years of age
B.   Collecting personal information from children under 13 years of age
C.   Displaying a picture of a child after obtaining verifiable parental consent
D.   Operating a website that is geared towards children in the United States with servers located outside the United States

ANSWER: B. Generally, COPPA applies to the online collection of personal information from children under 13 years of age. COPPA details what a website operator must include in a privacy policy, when and how to seek verifiable consent from a parent or guardian, and what responsibilities an operator has to protect children's privacy and safety online, including restrictions on marketing to those under the age of 13.

52. Which of the following is one of the main purposes of the Fair Credit Reporting Act ("FCRA")?

A. Give employers the right to correct credit reports for their employees
B. Encourage the dissemination of consumer data to foreign companies with a need to know the data
C. Limit the use of consumer reports to permissible purposes
D. Allow data reporters to place a debt on a consumer's credit report if they have a reasonable suspicion of the debt

ANSWER: C. Under the FCRA, a credit report (a type of consumer report) may only be acquired for a "permissible purpose." Section 604 of the FCRA sets forth the circumstances that are considered permissible, including (1) for employment, credit, license, or insurance purposes; and (2) with the written instructions of the consumer to whom the credit report relates.

53. Which of the following is an example of personal information from a public record?

A. Heath plan number from an insurance card
B. Name and address of an owner of a piece of real estate from a real estate deed
C. Driver's license number from a government issued citation
D. Genetic information from a private genome project

ANSWER: B. Public records are information collected and maintained by the government and that are available to the public. Public records include real estate deeds, birth and marriage certificates, tax liens, and other data recorded by the government and made available for public inspection.

54. Which of the following may be considered personal information?

A. Financial data of an organization
B. Intellectual property of an organization
C. Operational data of an organization
D. Human resources data of an organization

ANSWER: D. Financial data, intellectual property, and operational data are all important types of information related to an organization. However, personal information is only that information describing an identified or identifiable individual (in contrast to an organization). Human resources data describes the employees of an organization and therefore may constitute personal information because employees are individuals. All the other types of information listed describe the organization itself and are not types of personal information.

55. Which of the following would be classified as a deceptive trade practice by the FTC?

A. A website's privacy notice clearly states that it will not encrypt sensitive personal information, and the website does not, in fact, encrypt the data

B. An organization promises to honor opt-out requests within 10 days but fails to honor opt-out requests.

C. A rogue employee steals credit card information even though the organization took reasonable precautions to protect the credit card information

D. A bank does not comply with a regulation prohibiting the bank from revealing information about its customers

ANSWER: B. If an organization fails to comply with its privacy notice, it may be held liable by the FTC for a deceptive trade practice under Section 5 of the FTC Act, which prohibits "unfair or deceptive acts or practices in or affecting commerce." When companies tell consumers they will safeguard their personal information, the FTC can and does take law enforcement action to make sure that companies live up these promises. A violation of a promise made in a privacy notice is an example of a deceptive trade practice. Answer A would be an example of an unfair trade practice. The organization is not being deceptive, but the potential harm caused by the website's failure to encrypt sensitive data clearly outweighs the cost of providing encryption, a commonplace and inexpensive security control. Answer C would not be a deceptive trade practice because the organization had reasonable security measures in place, and the employee simply committed a crime. Answer D is incorrect because the FTC has no jurisdiction over banks and common carriers, which are under the supervision of other governmental agencies.

56.   The FTC recently classified which of the following activities as a deceptive trade practice?

A.   A patent assertion entity sending letters with misrepresentations to thousands of small businesses stating that they were infringing patents related to digital copiers

B.   A used car salesman making verbal misrepresentations about the quality of a car he was selling

C.   A postal carrier intentionally delivering mail to the wrong address

D.   A bank failing to insure all cash deposits

ANSWER: A. The FTC recently filed a complaint against a patent assertion entity that bought patents relating to digital copiers and then sent letters with misrepresentations to thousands of small businesses stating that they were infringing the patent and should purchase a patent license. The consent order agreed to by the patent assertion entity required it to refrain from making certain deceptive representations when asserting patent rights, such as false or unsubstantiated representations that a patent has been licensed in substantial numbers or has been licensed at particular prices. It also prohibited misrepresentations that a lawsuit will be initiated and about the imminence of such a lawsuit.

57. Which branch of the U.S. government is responsible for enforcing laws?

    A. Legislative
    B. Executive
    C. Judicial
    D. Administrative

ANSWER: B. The U.S. Constitution is the supreme law of the United States. It separates the United States government into three main powers, or branches. The legislative branch makes the laws, the executive branch enforces the laws, and the judicial branch evaluates and interprets the laws. The rationale for the separate branches is to ensure that no one person can have too much control of the government, thereby creating a separation of powers.

58. Which of the following is a type of agreement issued by an administrative agency in which the defendant agrees to stop the alleged illegal activity without admitting fault?

    A. Subpoena
    B. Judgment
    C. Consent decree
    D. National security letter

ANSWER: C. A consent decree is a formal document stating specific steps an entity needs to perform to rectify an alleged violation. When entering into a consent decree, the charged entity typically does not admit fault or liability. This is an important aspect of a consent decree: the alleged violator does not admit to any wrong-doing. This is beneficial to the charged entity because the decree cannot be used as evidence of fault in any other civil action that may be brought by those harmed by the unfair or deceptive practice. Many organizations prefer a consent decree for this reason and because they avoid a prolonged trial and the negative publicity associated with a trial.

59. Which of the following in a statute enables an individual to directly bring a lawsuit against a person who violates the statute?

   A. Private right of action
   B. Confidentiality provision
   C. Preemption clause
   D. Indemnity provision

ANSWER: A. A private right of action is a clause in a statute that expressly permits a private party or individual to bring a lawsuit against a person who violates the statute and causes harm to the private party.

60. Which of the following is the primary mechanism that the FTC uses to enforce privacy laws?

   A. Civil litigation
   B. Criminal litigation
   C. Administrative enforcement action
   D. Declaratory judgments

ANSWER: C. When the FTC believes that a person or company has committed an unfair or deceptive trade practice, it starts an investigation of the practice. Following the investigation, the FTC may initiate an enforcement action against the person or organization if it has "reason to believe" that the law is being, or has been, violated. An administrative enforcement action begins with the FTC issuing a complaint setting forth its charges. Enforcement actions are the primary mechanism by which the FTC enforces privacy laws.

61. Which of the following is arguably the most important law protecting privacy in the United States because of its broad scope?

A. Section 5 of the FTC Act
B. Children's Online Privacy Protection Act ("COPPA")
C. Foreign Intelligence Surveillance Act ("FISA")
D. Communications Assistance for Law Enforcement Act ("CALEA")

ANSWER: A. Section 5 of the FTC Act prohibits "unfair or deceptive acts or practices in or affecting commerce." It is a law that applies to a broad range of circumstances and affords the FTC broad discretion to enforce privacy rights. The other laws listed are quite specific and limited to protecting privacy in specific circumstances.

62. Which of the following is not a right set forth in the Consumer Privacy Bill of Rights introduced by the Obama administration?

A. Access and accuracy
B. Transparency
C. Security
D. Simplicity

ANSWER: D. In 2012, the Obama administration released a report titled "Consumer Data Privacy in a Networked World: A Framework for Protecting Privacy and Promoting Innovation in the Global Economy." The report contains a Consumer Privacy Bill of Rights, which include (1) Individual Control; (2) Transparency; (3) Respect for Context; (4) Security; (5) Access and Accuracy; (6) Focused Collection; and (7) Accountability. Simplicity is not one of the rights mentioned.

63.   Which of the following is an example of a self-regulatory organization?

   A.   PCI Security Standards Council
   B.   Office of the Comptroller of the Currency
   C.   Office of Thrift Supervision
   D.   The National Credit Union Administration

ANSWER: A. The PCI Security Standards Council is the organization responsible for the development, management, education, and awareness of the PCI Security Standards, including the Data Security Standard ("PCI DSS"). The Council therefore acts as a self-regulatory organization for the payment card processing industry. The Council's five founding global payment brands – American Express, Discover Financial Services, JCB International, MasterCard, and Visa Inc. – have agreed to incorporate the PCI DSS as the technical requirements of each of their data security compliance programs. The PCI DSS was developed to encourage and enhance cardholder data security and facilitate the broad adoption of consistent data security measures globally. PCI DSS applies to all entities involved in payment card processing, including merchants, processors, acquirers, issuers, and service providers, as well as all other entities that store, process or transmit cardholder data.

64. Which of the following organizations promotes cross-border information sharing and enforcement efforts for privacy authorities across the world?

A. International Organization for Standardization ("ISO")
B. Asia-Pacific Economic Cooperation ("APEC")
C. Global Privacy Enforcement Network ("GPEN")
D. Union of International Associations ("UIA")

ANSWER: C. The Global Privacy Enforcement Network ("GPEN") is an international network of privacy enforcement authorities tasked with aiding the flow of personal information across borders. In addition, GPEN supports joint enforcement initiatives and awareness campaigns related to privacy issues. The Federal Communications Commission ("FCC") and Federal Trade Commission ("FTC") are members of GPEN for the United States. Although APEC does have a cross border privacy enforcement arrangement, it is limited to APEC economies and is not worldwide in scope.

65. Which of the following are types of risk associated with the improper use of personal information?

A. Statutory risk and environmental risk
B. Legal risk and implicit risk
C. Legal risk and reputational risk
D. Investment risk and inherent risk

ANSWER: C. There are many benefits and risks associated with using personal information at an organization. An obvious benefit is the ability to create a more personalized experience for your users. For example, an online dating website may use personal information to help match its users based on age, gender, and personal preferences. There are four primary types of risk associated with the use of personal information. They are (1) legal risk, (2) operational risk, (3) reputational risk, and (4) investment risk.

66. Which of the following is NOT a major step when developing an effective information management program?

A. Discover
B. Build
C. Communicate
D. Compensate

ANSWER: D. The basic steps to developing an information management program are (1) discover, (2) build, (3) communicate, and (4) evolve. First, the organization must discover the environment in which the organization operates. For example, an organization should understand which laws regulate the organization and impose obligations on the organization related to privacy. An organization must also discover and develop its goals for the information management program. Next, the organization should build and design the information management program with the identified goals in mind. Typically, an information management program consists of policies and procedures related to how information will be managed at the organization. The third step is to communicate the policies and procedures to the employees of the organization. In some instances, a formal training may be required. Finally, the organization should ensure that the program evolves as the business needs and legal environment changes. By adhering to these four basic steps, an organization will develop an effective information management program.

67.   The Health Insurance Portability and Accountability Act ("HIPAA") applies to whom?

   A.   Domestic health institutions
   B.   Covered entities and their business associates
   C.   Book publishers of medical information
   D.   Domestic financial institutions

ANSWER: B. HIPAA was enacted in 1996 to define policies, procedures and guidelines that "covered entities" must adhere to for maintaining the privacy and security of individually identifiable protected health information ("PHI"). Covered entities generally include healthcare clearinghouses, employer sponsored health plans, health insurers, and healthcare providers. In 2009, the Health Information Technology for Economic and Clinical Health

("HITECH") Act expanded HIPAA's Privacy and Security Rules to directly regulate "business associates" of covered entities. Therefore, today HIPAA applies to both covered entities and their business associates.

68. What was the original purpose of the Health Insurance Portability and Accountability Act ("HIPAA")?

A. To improve the efficiency and effectiveness of the health care system
B. To mandate affordable healthcare for all citizens of the United States
C. To protect sensitive health information
D. To prevent pharmaceutical companies from charging unfair prices for lifesaving medication

ANSWER: A. HIPAA was originally enacted to improve the efficiency and effectiveness of the health care system. Specifically, HIPAA included Administrative Simplification provisions that required the U.S. Department of Health and Human Services ("HHS") to adopt national standards for electronic health care transactions and medical data code sets, unique health identifiers, and security. At the same time, Congress recognized that advances in electronic technology could erode the privacy of health information. Consequently, Congress incorporated into HIPAA provisions that mandated the adoption of federal privacy protections for individually identifiable health information.

69. Which of the following is NOT mandated by the Privacy Rule of the Health Insurance Portability and Accountability Act ("HIPAA")?

A. Covered entities with a direct treatment relationship with a patient must provide the patient with a privacy notice before the first service encounter

B. Covered entities must use and disclose protected health information for treatment, payment, and healthcare operations

C. Covered entities must train all workforce members on its privacy policies and procedures, as necessary and appropriate for them to carry out their functions

D. A covered entity must maintain reasonable and appropriate administrative, technical, and physical safeguards to prevent intentional or unintentional use or disclosure of protected health information

ANSWER: B. In accordance with the Privacy Rule, a covered entity is permitted, but not required, to use and disclose protected health information, without an individual's authorization, for the following purposes or situations: (1) to the individual; (2) treatment, payment, and healthcare operations; (3) opportunity to agree or object; (4) incident to an otherwise permitted use and disclosure; (5) public interest and benefit activities; and (6) limited data set for the purposes of research, public health or health care operations. Therefore, B is the correct answer because there are other permitted uses besides for treatment, payment, and health care operations. In addition, the Privacy Rule permits covered entities to disclose or use protected health information in certain circumstances but never requires disclosure or use.

Covered entities may rely on professional ethics and best judgments in deciding which of the permissive uses and disclosures to make. The HIPAA Privacy Rule also requires covered entities to implement appropriate administrative, technical, and physical safeguards to protect the privacy of protected health information ("PHI").

70. Which of the following is NOT a type of safeguard mandated by the Security Rule of the Health Insurance Portability and Accountability Act ("HIPAA")?

A. Technical
B. Administrative
C. Physical
D. Procedural

ANSWER: D. The Security Rule establishes national standards to protect individuals' electronic personal health information that is created, received, used, or maintained by a covered entity. The Security Rule requires appropriate administrative, physical, and technical safeguards to ensure the confidentiality, integrity, and security of electronic protected health information.

71.   Which of the following types of information is NOT protected by the Genetic Information Nondiscrimination Act ("GINA")?

   A.   The results of an individual's genetic tests
   B.   The manifestation of a disease or disorder in family members
   C.   A request for, or receipt of, genetic services
   D.   Sex or age of an individual

ANSWER: D. GINA prohibits discrimination in health coverage and employment based on genetic information. The statute defines "genetic information" as information encompassing: (1) an individual's genetic tests (including genetic tests done as part of a research study); (2) genetic tests of the individual's family members (defined as dependents and up to and including fourth degree relatives); (3) genetic tests of any fetus of an individual or family member who is a pregnant woman, and genetic tests of any embryo legally held by an individual or family member utilizing assisted reproductive technology; (4) the manifestation of a disease or disorder in family members (family history); and (5) any request for, or receipt of, genetic services or participation in clinical research that includes genetic services (genetic testing, counselling, or education) by an individual or family member. Under GINA, genetic information does not include information about the sex or age of an individual.

72.   Which of the following agencies is NOT responsible for enforcing a violation of the Genetic Information Nondiscrimination Act ("GINA")?

A.   Department of Labor
B.   Department of Health and Human Services ("HSS")
C.   Equal Employment Opportunity Commission ("EEOC")
D.   Federal Trade Commission ("FTC")

ANSWER: D. GINA is enforced by various federal agencies. The Department of Labor, the Department of the Treasury, and the Department of Health and Human Services are responsible for Title I of GINA, and the Equal Employment Opportunity Commission is responsible for Title II of GINA. Remedies for violations include corrective action and monetary penalties. Under Title II of GINA, individuals also have the right to pursue private litigation. The FTC does not enforce GINA.

73.   The Genetic Information Nondiscrimination Act ("GINA") prohibits discrimination based on genetic information for which type of insurance?

A.   Life insurance
B.   Disability insurance
C.   Long-term care insurance
D.   Health insurance

ANSWER: D. GINA prohibits discrimination in health coverage and employment based on the genetic information. GINA's health coverage non-discrimination protections do not extend to life insurance, disability insurance and long-term care insurance.

74.   In accordance with the Fair Credit Reporting Act ("FCRA"), what is an investigative consumer report?

   A.   Factual information on a consumer's credit record obtained directly from a creditor of the consumer or from a consumer reporting agency
   B.   A consumer report containing information about a consumer's past employment
   C.   A consumer report containing information on a consumer's character, general reputation, personal characteristics, or mode of living that is obtained through personal interviews
   D.   A report generated by a third-party investigator relating to a consumer's health

ANSWER: C. The FCRA defines an investigative consumer report as "a consumer report or portion thereof in which information on a consumer's character, general reputation, personal characteristics, or mode of living is obtained through personal interviews with neighbors, friends, or associates of the consumer reported on or with others with whom he is acquainted or who may have knowledge concerning any such items of information."

75. Which of the following is NOT a permissible purpose for a consumer reporting agency to furnish a consumer report?

A. In accordance with the written instructions of the consumer to whom it relates
B. To a person who intends to use the information in connection with a credit transaction involving the consumer
C. In response to an order of a court
D. For verification of eligibility for Social Security

ANSWER: D. A consumer reporting agency may only furnish a consumer report if a permissible purpose exists. The following are examples of permissible purposes: (1) in response to the order of a court having jurisdiction to issue such an order, or a subpoena issued in connection with proceedings before a federal grand jury; (2) in accordance with the written instructions of the consumer to whom it relates; and (3) to a person who intends to use the information either in connection with a credit transaction, employment purposes, the underwriting of insurance, or eligibility for a license.

76. When enforcing the Gramm-Leach-Bliley Act ("GLBA"), how does the FTC interpret the term "financial institution"?

A. A business that is significantly engaged in financial activities
B. A lender regulated by federal banking laws
C. A bank operating in the United States
D. A business whose main function is to lend money

ANSWER: A. In the GLBA, "financial institution" is defined as "any institution the business of which is engaging in financial activities." The FTC, however, interprets the term to only cover businesses "significantly engaged" in financial activities. Examples of such businesses include mortgage lenders, loan brokers, and check-cashing businesses.

77.   An educational institution may disclose which of the following pieces of information about its students as directory information?

    A.   Sexual orientation
    B.   Social security number
    C.   Address
    D.   Income

ANSWER: C. In accordance with the Family Educational Rights and Privacy Act ("FERPA"), schools may disclose, without consent, "directory" information such as a student's name, address, telephone number, date and place of birth, honors and awards, and dates of attendance. However, schools must tell parents and eligible students about the disclosure of directory information and allow parents and eligible students a reasonable amount of time to request that the school not disclose directory information about them (that is, provide them the opportunity to opt-out).

78.   The Telemarketing Sales Rule defines "telemarketing" as which of the following?

A.   An automated telephone call to a consumer for the purposes of effectuating a sale
B.   A plan, program, or campaign to induce the purchase of goods or services or a charitable contribution involving more than one interstate telephone call
C.   The solicitation of goods or services through one or more telephones
D.   A plan or program to induce the purchase of goods (excluding charitable contributions) involving more than one interstate telephone call

ANSWER: B. The Telemarketing Sales Rule (as amended) regulates "telemarketing" – defined in the Rule as "a plan, program, or campaign . . . to induce the purchase of goods or services or a charitable contribution" involving more than one interstate telephone call. With some important exceptions, any business or individual that takes part in "telemarketing" must comply with the Rule. This is true whether, as "telemarketers," they initiate or receive telephone calls to or from consumers, or as "sellers," they provide, offer to provide, or arrange to provide goods or services to consumers in exchange for payment. It makes no difference whether a company makes or receives calls using low-tech equipment or the newest technology – such as voice response units and other automated systems. Similarly, it makes no difference whether the calls are made from outside the United States; so long as they are made to consumers in the United States, those making the calls, unless otherwise exempt, must comply with the Rule's provisions. If the calls are made to induce the purchase of goods, services, or a charitable contribution, the company is engaging in "telemarketing."

79. What was the primary purpose for creating the National Do Not Call Registry?

A. To mandate affirmative consumer consent before any entity may conduct a telemarketing call
B. To prohibit telemarketing calls placed late at night or during dinner time
C. To prohibit all telemarketing calls
D. To offer consumers a choice regarding telemarketing calls

ANSWER: D. The National Do Not Call Registry is a list of phone numbers from consumers who have indicated their preference to limit the telemarketing calls they receive. The registry is managed by the Federal Trade Commission ("FTC"), the nation's primary consumer protection agency. It is enforced by the FTC, the Federal Communications Commission ("FCC"), and various state officials. The national registry was created in 2003 to offer consumers a choice regarding telemarketing calls.

80. Which of the following types of calls are NOT regulated by the National Do Not Call Registry?

A. Calls to consumers living in Puerto Rico and the District of Columbia
B. Automated telephone calls
C. Calls from political organizations, charities, telephone surveyors, or companies with which a consumer has an existing business relationship
D. Calls made manually without the assistance of an automated dialer

ANSWER: C. The National Do Not Call Registry does not cover calls from political organizations, charities, telephone surveyors, or companies with which a consumer has an existing business relationship. The area codes in the National Do Not Call Registry cover the 50 states, the District of Columbia, Puerto Rico, U.S. Virgin Islands, Guam, North Mariana Islands, American Samoa, and toll-free numbers. It makes no difference whether a company makes or receives calls using low-tech equipment or the newest technology – such as voice response units and other automated systems. Similarly, it makes no difference whether the calls are made from outside the United States; so long as they are made to consumers in the United States, those making the calls, unless otherwise exempt, must comply with the Rule's provisions.

81. If a third-party telemarketer acting on behalf of a charity calls a consumer, how may the consumer prevent the third-party telemarketer from calling him again in the future?

A. Register his phone number with the National Do Not Call Registry
B. Call the local police department and file a formal complaint
C. File a formal complaint with the Federal Bureau of Investigation
D. Specifically ask the third-party telemarketer not to call again and to place his number on the telemarketer's entity-specific do not call list

ANSWER: D. Charities that are calling on their own behalf to solicit charitable contributions are not covered by the requirements of the national registry. However, if a third-party telemarketer is calling on behalf of a charity, a consumer may ask not to receive any more calls from or on behalf of that specific charity and be placed on the telemarketer's entity-specific suppression list. If a third-party telemarketer calls again on behalf of that charity, the telemarketer may be subject to a fine of up to $16,000.

82. A company with an existing business relationship with a consumer may call the consumer for up to how long after the consumer's last purchase?

A. 12 months
B. 18 months
C. 24 months
D. There is no limit so long as there is an existing business relationship

ANSWER: B. In accordance with the Telemarketing Sales Rule, a company with which a consumer has an established business relationship may call for up to 18 months after the consumer's last purchase or last delivery, or last payment, unless the consumer asks the company not to call again. In that case, the company must honor the request not to call.

83. When requesting a consumer's consent to make unsolicited pre-recorded telemarketing calls ("robocalls") to the consumer, what standard is used to evaluate the propriety of the notice?

A. Reasonable
B. Clear and convincing
C. Clear and conspicuous
D. Beyond a reasonable doubt

ANSWER: C. A consumer's written consent to receive telemarketing robocalls (unsolicited pre-recorded telemarketing calls) must be signed and be sufficient to show that the consumer: (1) received "clear and conspicuous disclosure" of the consequences of providing the requested consent (that is, the consumer will receive future calls that deliver pre-recorded messages by or on behalf of a specific seller); and (2) having received this information, the consumer agrees unambiguously to receive such calls at a telephone number the consumer designates. In addition, the written agreement must be obtained "without requiring, directly or indirectly, that the agreement be executed as a condition of purchasing any good or service."

84.   The CAN-SPAM Act applies to what type of electronic messages?

   A.   Where the secondary purpose of the message is transactional
   B.   Where the secondary purpose of the message is commercial
   C.   Where the primary purpose of the message is transactional
   D.   Where the primary purpose of the message is commercial

ANSWER: D. Despite its name, the CAN-SPAM Act doesn't apply just to bulk email. It covers all commercial messages, which the law defines as "any electronic mail message the primary purpose of which is the commercial advertisement or promotion of a commercial product or service," including email that promotes content on commercial websites.

85.   How promptly must businesses that send
      unsolicited commercial emails process opt-out
      requests received from consumers?

   A.   7 days
   B.   10 days
   C.   30 days
   D.   45 days

ANSWER: B. In accordance with the CAN-SPAM Act,
businesses must honor a recipient's opt-out request
within 10 business days. Businesses are not allowed
to charge a fee, require the recipient give any
personally identifying information beyond an email
address, or make the recipient take any step other
than sending a reply email or visiting a single page on
an Internet website as a condition for honoring an
opt-out request. In addition, businesses must
continue to process opt-out requests for at least 30
days after transmission of a commercial message.

86.   An operator of which of the following is
      regulated by the Children's Online Privacy
      Protection Act ("COPPA")?

   A.   A general audience website that provides
        online games
   B.   A mobile application for paying utility bills
   C.   A social networking service directed to
        children over 13
   D.   A general audience website that provides
        online games when the operator has
        knowledge that the games are being played
        by children under the age of 13

ANSWER: D. Congress enacted COPPA in 1998. COPPA required the Federal Trade Commission ("FTC") to issue and enforce regulations concerning children's online privacy. The primary goal of COPPA is to place parents in control over what information is collected from their young children online. COPPA applies to (1) operators of commercial websites and online services (including mobile apps) directed to children under the age of 13 that collect, use, or disclose personal information from children, and (2) operators of general audience websites or online services with actual knowledge that they are collecting, using, or disclosing personal information from children under the age of 13.

87. Which of the following is NOT regulated by the Children's Online Privacy Protection Act ("COPPA")?

    A.   Online contact information
    B.   A screen name that functions as online contact information
    C.   A photograph of a child
    D.   Pornography

ANSWER: D. The Federal Trade Commission ("FTC") has defined personal information in its Rule implementing COPPA to include: (1) first and last name; (2) a home or other physical address including street name and name of a city or town; (3) online contact information; (4) a screen or user name that functions as online contact information; (5) a telephone number; (6) a social security number; (7) a persistent identifier that can be used to recognize a user over time and across different websites or online services; (8) a photograph, video, or audio file, where such file contains a child's image or voice; (9) geolocation information sufficient to identify street name and name of a city or town; or (10) information concerning the child or the parents of that child that the operator collects online from the child and combines with an identifier described above. COPPA was not designed to protect children from viewing particular types of content, such as pornography. If parents are concerned about their children accessing online pornography or other inappropriate materials, they should consider a filtering program or an internet service provider that offers tools to help screen out or restrict access to such material.

88. May an operator of a general audience website rely on age information submitted by its users to determine if it must comply with the Children's Online Privacy Protection Act ("COPPA")?

A. No, COPPA applies to all general audience websites with users under the age of 13

B. No, an operator will be deemed to have knowledge of the true age of all website users regardless of user-submitted age information

C. Yes, the operator may rely on user-submitted age information unless he has actual knowledge that a child under the age of 13 is using the website

D. Yes, the operator may rely on user-submitted age information even if he has actual knowledge that children under the age of 13 are using the website

ANSWER: C. COPPA covers operators of general audience websites or online services only when such operators have actual knowledge that a child under the age of 13 is the person providing personal information. The Rule does not require operators to ask the age of visitors. However, an operator of a general audience site or service that chooses to screen its users for age in a neutral fashion may rely on the age information its users enter, even if that age information is not accurate. In some circumstances, this may mean that children are able to register on a site or service in violation of the operator's Terms of Service. If, however, the operator later determines that a particular user is a child under the age of 13, COPPA's notice and parental consent requirements will be triggered.

89. Violations of the Children's Online Privacy Protection Act ("COPPA") may result in a civil fine of how much per violation?

A. $1,000
B. $10,000
C. $16,000
D. $100,000

ANSWER: C. A court can hold operators who violate COPPA liable for civil penalties of up to $16,000 per violation. The amount of civil penalties a court assesses depends on a number of factors, including the egregiousness of the violations, whether the operator has previously violated the Rule, the number of children involved, the amount and type of personal information collected, how the information was used, whether it was shared with third parties, and the size of the company.

90.   The California Online Privacy Protection Act ("CalOPPA") was amended in 2013 to address what issue?

A.   Online tracking
B.   Social networking
C.   Unsolicited commercial email
D.   Credit card fraud

ANSWER: A. CalOPPA was the first law in the nation to require operators of commercial web sites and online services to post a privacy policy. CalOPPA applies to operators of commercial web sites and online services that collect personally identifiable information about Californians. It requires them to say what they do and do what they say (that is, to conspicuously post a privacy policy and to comply with it). The Act was amended in 2013 to address the issue of online tracking (that is, the collection of personal information about consumers as they move across web sites and online services).

91.   The Privacy Protection Act ("PPA") protects which of the following?

A.   A promotional flyer created by a religious institution
B.   An article written by a student at an educational institution for internal dissemination
C.   Documentary material held by a journalist
D.   A book published by the government

ANSWER: C. The Privacy Protection Act ("PPA") was enacted in 1980 to protect journalists and newsrooms from searches by government officials. Specifically, the Act prohibits "a government officer or employee, in connection with the investigation or prosecution of a criminal offense, to search for or seize any work product materials possessed by a person reasonably believed to have a purpose to disseminate to the public a newspaper, book, broadcast, or other similar form of public communication." The Act protects both work product and documentary materials. To search or seize protected material, the government is generally first required to obtain a subpoena from a court on the basis that there is probable cause to believe that the person possessing the materials has committed or is committing a criminal offense to which the materials relate. Search or seizure without a court order is permitted only if immediate seizure of the materials is necessary to prevent death or serious bodily injury.

92.   When may the government rightfully seize work product materials from a journalist?

   A.   When there is reason to believe that the seizure of the materials may prevent harm
   B.   When there is probable cause to believe that the journalist has committed a criminal offense to which the materials relate
   C.   When the source of the materials has provided consent
   D.   Never; the work product of a journalist is unconditionally protected

ANSWER: B.   The Privacy Protection Act ("PPA") was enacted in 1980 to protect journalists and newsrooms from searches by government officials. The PPA provides two general exceptions to its protections: (1) when there is probable cause to believe that the person possessing such materials has committed or is committing the criminal offense to which the materials relate and (2) there is reason to believe that the immediate seizure of such materials is necessary to prevent the death of, or serious bodily injury to, a human being. General notions of "harm" are not enough. The exception requires serious bodily injury or death.

93. What standard must be satisfied before the government may install a pen register on a telephone line for surveillance purposes?

    A. The information likely to be obtained is relevant to an ongoing criminal investigation
    B. Probable cause exists that the person using the line has committed a crime
    C. Specific and articulable facts justifying the use of the pen register
    D. The use of a pen register does not constitute a search and therefore may be freely installed by the government

ANSWER: A. A pen register is a device which records or decodes electronic or other impulses which identify the numbers called or otherwise transmitted on the telephone line to which such device is installed. While a pen register records only outgoing phone numbers dialled, a "trap and trace" device logs incoming phone numbers. If a court finds that the attorney for the government has adequately certified to the court that the information likely to be obtained by installation of a pen register or trap and trace device is relevant to an ongoing criminal investigation, the court shall enter an order authorizing the installation and use of the device.

94. Which of the following is NOT a primary impact of the USA PATRIOT Act?

A. Enhancing the federal government's capacity to share intelligence
B. Strengthening the criminal laws against terrorism
C. Removing obstacles to investigating terrorism
D. Preventing foreign nationals from traveling to the United States

ANSWER: D. The Department of Justice's 2004 field report on the USA PATRIOT Act sets forth the following four primary impacts of the Act: (1) enhancing the federal government's capacity to share intelligence; (2) strengthening the criminal laws against terrorism; (3) removing obstacles to investigating terrorism; and (4) updating the law to reflect new technology.

95. In civil litigation, what is the appropriate mechanism for a party to contest the scope of a discovery request seeking confidential information that would cause serious injury to the party if disclosed?

A. Motion to compel
B. Subpoena
C. Protective order
D. Judgment on the merits

ANSWER: C. A court may, for good cause, issue a protective order to protect a party or person from annoyance, embarrassment, oppression or undue burden or expense. In evaluating requests for protective orders, courts have considered various factors, including, the confidentiality interests at issue, the need to protect public health and safety, the fairness and efficiency of entering a protective order, and the importance of the litigation to the public.

96.   Which of the following should be redacted from a document before it is filed with a federal court?

    A.   All but the last four digits of a Social Security or taxpayer-identification number
    B.   All financial accounts numbers
    C.   A minor's initials
    D.   The date of birth of a party

ANSWER: A. Rule 5.2 of the Federal Rules of Civil Procedure states that both electronic and paper filings made with the court should only include (1) the last four digits of the Social Security number and taxpayer-identification number; (2) the year of the individual's birth; (3) a minor's initials; and (4) the last four digits of a financial account number. Therefore, a party should redact all but the last four digits of a Social Security or taxpayer-identification number from a document before it is filed with a federal court.

97.   Domestic financial institutions are required to provide an annual privacy notice to which of the following?

   A.   Consumers
   B.   Customers
   C.   Employees
   D.   Contractors

ANSWER: B. The Gramm–Leach–Bliley Act ("GLBA"), also known as the "Financial Services Modernization Act," was enacted in 1999. It applies to institutions that are significantly engaged in financial activities in the United States (also known as "domestic financial institutions"). In accordance with the Privacy Rule, domestic financial institutions are require to provide an initial privacy notice when the <u>customer</u> relationship is established and annually thereafter.

98.   Domestic financial institutions are required to provide the customer with the opportunity to opt out of sharing what type of information with unaffiliated third-parties?

   A.   Personal information
   B.   Publicly available information
   C.   Non-public personal information
   D.   De-identified personal information

ANSWER: C. The Gramm-Leach-Bliley Act ("GLBA") requires domestic financial institutions to provide opt-out notice prior to sharing non-public personal information ("NPI") with unaffiliated third parties. NPI includes any personally identifiable financial information that a financial institution collects about an individual in connection with providing a financial product or service, unless that information is otherwise publicly available. Examples of NPI include a customer's name, address, income, social security number, and other account related information, such as account numbers, payment history, loan or deposit balances, and credit or debit card purchases.

99.   The Gramm-Leach-Bliley Act ("GLBA") prohibits which of the following practices?

A.   Sharing of personal information
B.   Transfer of financial accounts to financial institutions located outside the United States
C.   Pretexting
D.   Lending of money to individuals residing overseas

ANSWER: C. The GLBA prohibits "pretexting" – the practice of obtaining customer information from financial institutions by false pretenses. Specifically, the Act prohibits any person from obtaining customer information relating to another person by making a false, fictitious, or fraudulent statement or representation to an employee or customer of a financial institution.

100. What are the primary mechanisms for financial institutions to comply with the Bank Secrecy Act?

A. Currency Transaction Reports and Suspicious Activity Reports
B. Currency Transaction Reports and Compliance Audits
C. Compliance Audits Suspicious Activity Reports
D. Information Security Audits and Compliance Reports

ANSWER: A. The Bank Secrecy Act of 1970, also known as the Currency and Foreign Transactions Reporting Act, requires financial institutions in the United States to assist government agencies to detect and prevent money laundering. Specifically, the act requires financial institutions to keep records of cash purchases of negotiable instruments, file reports of cash purchases of these negotiable instruments of more than $10,000 (daily aggregate amount), and report suspicious activity that might signify money laundering, tax evasion, or other criminal activities. Currency Transaction Reports ("CTRs") and Suspicious Activity Reports ("SARs") are the primary means used by banks to satisfy the requirements of the BSA.

Made in the USA
San Bernardino, CA
29 May 2015